Today's most authoritative and comprehensive guide to success in real estate development, building construction and renovation.

"Finally! A comprehensive tool for developers and builders, providing indispensable resources presented for today's market. 'GO / NO GO' is a dominant publication equipped for those who want to develop real estate or those who currently are developing real estate and wish to expand their knowledge with a neoteric perspective. Mark Noe dispenses his wise brand of developer information to an increasing audience of would-be and experienced developers and builders."

Lee Saylor
Saylor Consulting Group
San Francisco, CA

"Facts not frills about the development and construction process delivered in a make-sense, practical style. Mark Noe cuts through the mystery to the principles. You will make money by reading his book."

Michael Hesse, CCIM, CPM
Coldwell Banker Commercial Moore & Co.
Boulder, CO

"The book is very comprehensive and certainly is the most practical summary I ever have seen on the subject. Plus it serves as an excellent guide."

Michael D. Gainey, M.D.
Vascular Surgeon and Investor
Reno, NV

"My underwriting of commercial and residential construction loans up to $40,000,000 would be streamlined greatly if applicants and clients had the 'GO / NO GO' Financing Principles down pat. This also holds true of my associates."

Caroline Sjostedt, Vice President
US Bank
Walnut Creek, CA

"The outstanding and original publication, 'GO / NO GO', should be a GO for every real estate professional, builder and owner. Whether you have been in the real estate development or construction fields two months or two decades, this resource should be at your desk."

Charles M. Sink, Esq.
Farella, Braun & Martel
San Francisco, CA

FREE CONSULTING with book purchase ON ANY REAL ESTATE TOPIC
Call Mark Noe at (707) 938-2738 or (925) 939-8707
Proof of purchase required

Other topical works by Mark Noe:

"Managing Construction Claims
or Minimizing Potential For Litigation"

"Common Sense First Step Toward
Becoming Own Expert"

"Construction Contract Disputes
Can Be Minimized"

Mark Noe

About the Author

of Go/No Go

Mark Noe has developed or managed the development of over 2,000,000 square feet of buildings. A skilled consultant, he has helped scores of clients achieve success in their commercial, industrial and residential projects in more than seventy jurisdictions in California. He provides expert witness testimony on a wide range of real estate topics, including feasibility, valuations, industry standards of care, contracts, and construction defects.

Educated in Civil Engineering at Purdue and Stanford Universities, Noe has been a faculty member at the University of California Extension at Berkeley and Davis. At Golden Gate University, he chaired the Real Estate Advisory Committee of the Center for Professional Development, and teaches as a member of the Adjunct Faculty of the Graduate School of Business.

Seasoned in every aspect of real estate construction and development, Noe served more than a decade on the Walnut Creek Planning Commission, and as a Design Review Commission member and on the Civic Center Building Committee for that city.

A veteran developer, contract administrator and construction manager for real estate projects valued from $100,000 to $150,000,000, Noe's professional expertise is sought by corporations and private investors.

Memberships:
American Arbitration Association, Commercial Panelist and Member
Urban Land Institute, Academic Associate
Western Construction Consultants Association, Member

Go / No Go

**A Hands-On Guide to Successful Real Estate Development,
Building Construction and Renovation
From Concept Through Completion**

Go / No Go

A Hands-On Guide to Successful Real Estate Development,
Building Construction and Renovation
From Concept Through Completion

MARK NOE

 REMARK Publishing

This book reflects the views and experiences of the author, and only the author. **"Go / No Go"** is designed to provide information in regard to the subject matter covered. It is sold with the understanding that the publisher and author are not engaged in rendering legal or accounting services. If legal or other expert assistance is required, the services of a competent professional should be sought.

You are encouraged to learn as much as possible about real estate development, building construction and remodeling and tailor such information to your individual needs. For more information, see the many references noted throughout **"Go/No Go"**.

This text should be used only as a professional guide and not as the ultimate source of real estate development and building construction information.

If you do not wish to be bound by the above, you may return this book to the publisher for a full refund.

Published by:

REMARK Publishing
P.O. Box 2056
Sonoma, CA 95476-2056

Cover Design, Graphics and Typography: K.C. Kelly, John Hernikl and AnDee Williams
Copy Editing: Jill Keough, Susan Wyatt and Hugh Rudorf
Processing: Whiteley Enterprises

Copyright © 1999 by Mark W. Noe
First Printing 1999
Printed in the United States of America
ISBN: 0-9670010-0-5
Library of Congress Catalog No. 99-93241
E-mail address: copystore@vom.com
Website: www.westcon.org/noe/

"Don't let what you cannot do interfere with what you can do."
John Wooden; Legendary Basketball Hall of Famer

"Problems are opportunities in work clothes."
Henry J. Kaiser, Builder and Industrialist

"Take whatever you are blessed with in life and try and keep a shine on it."
"Life Its Ownself" by Sports Authority Dan Jenkins

To my parents, no longer with us, at least
in this planet, but certainly with me
in spirit. **"GO / NO GO"** is a primary result
of their unceasing encouragement to pursue
dreams and make them realities.

Table of Contents

Table of Contents

*or "MINIMIZING THE POTENTIAL FOR LITIGATION"

ACKNOWLEDGMENTS

This book originated as a private seminar on **"Project Feasibility"**, progressing and expanding to a series of courses at UC-Berkeley Extension, UC-Davis Extension and Golden Gate University Center for Professional Development, culminating in a Certificate Program in Real Estate Development at Golden Gate University. The energy and input from the hundreds of students participating in these classes were invaluable, and several of these skilled professionals provided significant contributions to the final **"GO / NO GO"** book, and are listed in the contributor acknowledgments below or in each section. My very sincere thanks for their efforts and for the others who wrote the timely articles and special reports which truly make **"GO / NO GO"** a unique guide to hands-on successful real estate development and building construction.

Special thanks are extended to Dr. Anthony D. Branch, Provost, Walnut Creek Campus, Golden Gate University for his support and encouragement when real estate interest and activity could best be defined as almost non-existent. Tony provided the energy and support for this topic to be taught as part of the Graduate School of Business, Department of Finance, at the Walnut Creek and Rohnert Park Campuses.

On a more personal note, I cannot give enough thanks for the efforts of Jill Keough and K.C. Kelly in putting this whole morass together into a professional format and putting up with my own peccadillos, and pushing for their own professional points of view, which usually (sigh!), were correct. And thanks, too, to Bill Ludwig for his prompt execution of the details and his own significant input. Thanks also to Paula Farwell and Ed Bell for their never-ending patience with my never-ending tedious questions.

Finally, kudos to my family in Phoenix, Arizona and in California. To Dave Noe, PE, in Phoenix for our construction conversations over the years and to Anne Noe for her and Dave's love and support; to Dr. John and Ann Noe in Sacramento and Laura and David Hoff in San Jose for all of the blessings, help and love which you have given me during the past years.

PROFESSIONAL CONTRIBUTORS

Gary D. Binger, Planning Director, ABAG [permit processing]
Caroline Sjostedt, Vice Pres., US Bank [financing]
Lawrence E. Hazard, SIOR, CRS Brokerage, [brokerage, marketing, leases]
Paul Richardson, Dir. Planning, City of Walnut Creek [permit processing]
Dr. Steve D. Ugbah, Professor Cal State-Hayward [market research]
Arthur F. Coon, Miller, Starr & Regalia [CEQA Process]
Michael H. Zischke, Landels, Ripley & Diamond [CEQA Process]
D. Bruce Moen, PE [Construction Management]
Deborah Rothstein, CPM [Property Management]
Paul N. Farthing [Appraisal]
Karl E. Geier, Miller, Starr & Regalia [Environmental Questionnaire]
Douglas Thompson, Penn Environmental [Environmental Site Assessments]

FEASIBILITY

P R E F A C E

The focus of this text is directed to residential <u>or</u> commercial "Middle Market Development"...Projects from $100k to $10M in scope: generally in the $2-5M range. **The principles discussed apply to both residential subdivisions and commercial or residential projects.** This may be a difficult concept to grasp initially, and if so, for now you will have to accept it on faith.

The process of real estate development is dynamic. All parts must mesh with each other, and there are two truths in real estate development. **First, there will be surprises....no matter how well you plan or how experienced you are. Second, there are "rules" to the process of development and no project is sacrosanct from the rules.** One of the purposes of this text is to aid in minimizing the surprises and gain knowledge of the rules.

A second purpose is to provide the tools whereby a project's feasibility may be analyzed at minimal cost (cash out of <u>your</u> pocket) and the third purpose is to know the questions to ask. **The "answers" for each project may vary, but the questions always will be pretty much the same.**

In today's complex and demanding real estate climate, even minor errors sometimes can torpedo a project, often with serious financial consequences for all of the players. This text, from a developer's or builder's perspective, focuses on the critical questions of a project's feasibility, and shows techniques to obtain the answers:

THE MARKET What is the width, breadth and seasoning of the market? What are the requirements of prospective tenants and buyers, and what is their motivation to make a decision? What is the marketing plan and who will implement it? Can the "good idea" project be financed?

THE ENTITLEMENT What are the strategies for working with planning staffs, planning commissions, regulatory agencies and community action groups? How do NIMBY complaints keep from escalating into WWIII?

THE COST <u>All</u> of the costs, not just the contractor's bid and the price of the land. **How can a reliable proforma be prepared when there are no drawings to bid?** How are contingent risks analyzed; and when should the cost analysis first be made?

Following are "Leadership Insights" culled and paraphrased from several significant developers: On advice for real estate developers and investors: Focus on fundamentals. Put the "real" back in real estate. Excercise prudent due-dilligence. Eschew "creative or engineered" financing to make the numbers work. Not only do developers and property owners need a good product, they need to set realistic and achievable financing, leasing or selling, design and management/operating goals.

There are a number of unique opportunities today in several micro-markets. **Remember that real estate development still works within a micro, not macro marketplace.** One cannot generalize about an industry's recovery when each market, submarket and micro-market has its own recovery timetable. If you build the right product in the right location with the right fundamentals, you will be successful. However, many still commit the biggest ego and judgement error of all: "I've never seen a piece of dirt I didn't like".

PREFACE (continued)

Finally, there are general and current economic considerations which appear to be meaningful and which may have important implications for your project:

1. The emotional impact of intangible value, particularly for residential projects, has been reduced. Generally, the "sticks and stones" value controls.

2. There is reliable consensus from competent sources that upwards of 20% of California's businesses still intend to relocate some or all of their operations outside of the state. The consensus of the same surveys indicates **that California lost some 800,000 jobs during the recession which most say ended in mid-1994.** Yet approximately 400,000 people (interstate and immigrants) still arrive in California annually.

3. There is evidence that the Baby Boom Generation is now entering a savings period as they plan for their children's education, their own retirement, and they have reduced their own spending significantly......a major portion of the buying binge which fueled the '80's. **For the first time in history (May '96) personal investment in the stock market and mutual funds, exceeded personal savings account funds.**

4. Equity has been required for Middle Market Development projects since the mid-'80's. This is not a new phenomenon!

5. Increased public and private awareness of real estate values, regulatory agencies, the S&L debacle, withdrawal of Pacific Rim funds, etc. have eliminated the takeout by "sucker syndications" of poorly planned or poorly performing projects. Truly, it's back to basic fundamentals. You can't count on being bailed out as in the past.

6. Don Bruzzone, President of California Development, Inc. coined his own "three strikes an' yer out" long before it was politically correct. Heed the advice!

> **Strike One: I'm going to build a monument**
> **Strike Two: I can build it cheaper (than anyone else)**
> **Strike Three: I make the market**

TWO THINGS TO REMEMBER
No. 1 - Real Estate Development is simple...not easy, but simple. Don't complicate it!
No. 2 - Don't forget Rule No. 1
TWO MORE THINGS TO REMEMBER
No. 3 - In the middle of difficulty lies opportunity.
> *Ralph Waldo Emerson*
No. 4 - Nothing will be attempted if all possible objections must first be overcome.
> *Samuel Johnson*

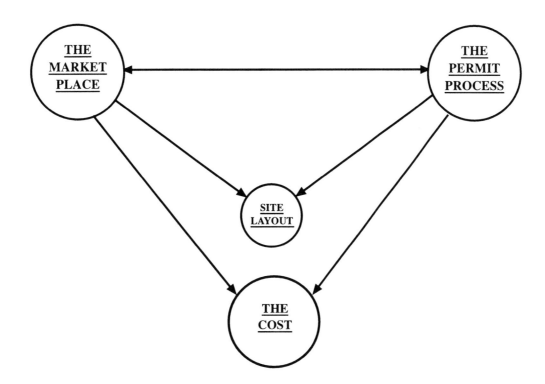

THE MARKET PLACE

Demographics
Competition; Price/Location
Current Absorption/Inventory
Site Identification/Evaluation
Market Rate [s]
For Sale or Lease?
Depth, Breadth, and Seasoning
      of Market
User Profile; Motivation and
      Requirements
Realistic Evaluation of Risk
Marketing Plan Implementation
      [by whom?] target decision-makers]
Community Profile/Attitude
Financeable?

THE PERMIT PROCESS

Entitlements to Use
General Plan/Specific Plan
Initial Study [agency form]
Hazardous Wastes
Environmental Concerns
Time to Process
Permit Fees [also under costs]
No. of Agencies to Approve
Community Action Groups
Heritage or Tree Preservation?
Attitude of Staff/Council
Utilities Available?
Off-Site Infrastructure [if any]
Dedications/Exactions [if any]
Convenants and Restrictions [if req'd]
History of Property

FEASIBILITY

PREFACE   (Continued)

THE COST

LAND COST
- Purchase Cost
- Title and Closing Costs
- Property Taxes for Holding Period

ORGANIZATIONAL COST
- Legal and Accounting
- Partnership/Venture Agreements

PRELIMINARY DESIGN COST
- Schematic/Preliminary Drawings (A&E)
- Soils Report
- Toxic Testing or Phase I Environmental
- Use Permit Fees
- Design Review Fees
- Other Consulting Fees

FINAL DESIGN COSTS
(incl. Development Fees)
- Final Working Drawings (A&E)
- Building Permit/Plan Check
- Acreage/Development Fees

BUILDING CONSTRUCTION COST
- Building Shell
- Tenant Improvements (TI's)
- Sitework/Utilities
- Project Supervision
- Developer's Fee/Project Management
- Contractor's Overhead & Profit
- Contingency

REAL ESTATE BROKERAGE COMMISSIONS
- For Leasing
- For Selling

CONSTRUCTION FINANCING COSTS
- Loan Points
- Appraisal Fee
- Title and Closing Costs
- ALTA Premium (if applicable)
- Interest During Construction
- Interest During Holding Period
- (Credit) for Income During Holding Period

PERMANENT FINANCING COSTS
- Loan Points
- Appraisal Fee
- Title and Closing Costs (short rate)
- ALTA Premium (if applicable)
- Mortgage Broker Fees
- Legal Fees

NOTE: Operating/Management Costs, if applicable, may be included in construction or permanent financing as appropriate

PROJECT IS A "GO"

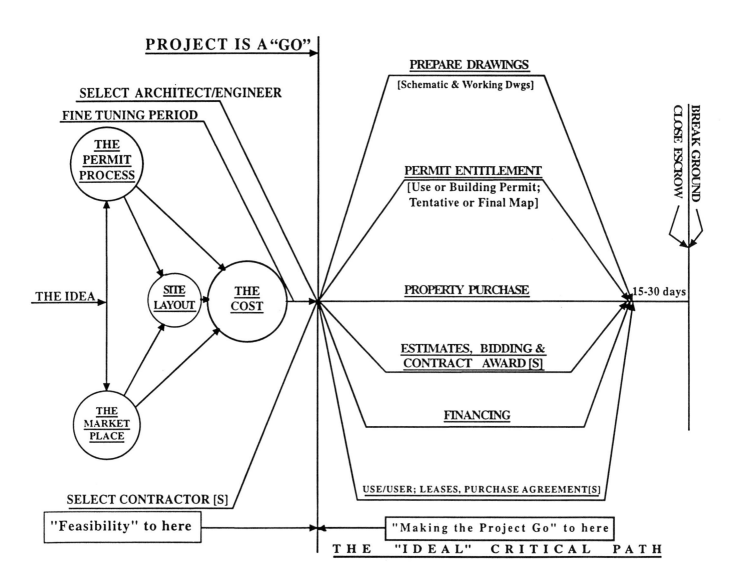

SELECT ARCHITECT/ENGINEER

FINE TUNING PERIOD

THE PERMIT PROCESS

THE IDEA

SITE LAYOUT

THE COST

THE MARKET PLACE

PREPARE DRAWINGS
[Schematic & Working Dwgs]

PERMIT ENTITLEMENT
[Use or Building Permit;
Tentative or Final Map]

PROPERTY PURCHASE

ESTIMATES, BIDDING &
CONTRACT   AWARD [S]

FINANCING

USE/USER; LEASES, PURCHASE AGREEMENT[S]

15-30 days

BREAK GROUND
CLOSE ESCROW

SELECT CONTRACTOR [S]

"Feasibility" to here

"Making the Project Go" to here

THE   "IDEAL" CRITICAL PATH

Project Feasibility:

The Developer's Perspective

FEASIBILITY

INTRODUCTION/OVERVIEW/BASIC ELEMENTS

Mainly, a real estate developer is a generalist...weaving through an intricate process with other professionals who provide specialized services within a particular area of expertise.....design, financing, construction and the like. The Urban Land Institute notes that "a developer cannot be expert in all aspects of the business. Instead, **successful developers know what questions to ask and whom to ask**; what to look for with respect to common practices, and standard rules of thumb".

Real Estate Development no longer is "a seat of the pants" business, if, in fact, it ever was. However, there still may be an intuitive gut feeling or a dream for a potential project which does work out in the face of overall negativity from the marketplace.

Learn and understand the rules of the Real Estate Development game. You may **not like** the rules, yet if you are going to be involved in the process, **you must know how the game is played! The same principles apply to residential and commercial projects; projects large or small...only the length of time and the number of zeroes are changed. THE PROCESS IS THE SAME.**

REAL ESTATE DEVELOPMENT AND BUILDING CONSTRUCTION HAS TO BE FUN....OR DON'T DO IT!

DEFINITIONS
Capitalization (Cap) Rate: The rate of return by which the marketplace values a particular type of real estate project. The cap rate is <u>divided into</u> the net annual income; <u>not multiplied</u> by the cost

Proforma Analysis: A financial, preliminary cost analysis of the <u>total</u> project cost, not merely the construction estimate or bids

Inventory: The amount of space or number of units available for a particular building type

Absorption: The amount of space or units consumed (sold or leased) within a finite period, usually one year

Value Added/Residual Value: Synergistic? May include intangibles as flexibility in design, quality and appearance, ease in identification. Thought through and understood with the end user in mind.

What value added is not: $100,000 land with a $200,000 building developed on it; sold for $300,000. "Value Added" <u>always</u> has a greater economic or emotional (as in residential) value than the "nuts and bolts" replacement value.

FEASIBILITY

BASIC ELEMENTS OF REAL ESTATE DEVELOPMENT (Inherent in every project)
and these elements may be all unfolding at the same time!
-Property to be Developed (LAND)
-Entitlement to Use (PERMIT PROCESSING)
-Source of Funds to Build (FINANCING)
-Use or Uses for the Property (MARKET RESEARCH, MARKETING)
-Design and Physical Construction (DESIGN/BUILD)

FACTS, BELIEFS, AND (MY) PHILOSOPHY IN REAL ESTATE DEVELOPMENT

1.   All developers have had financial difficulties at least once
2.   No large corporation (with other product) has stayed in development
3.   **Difficult to be both a contractor and developer** unless very large
4.   Development has a **micro, not a macro** marketplace
5.   Development is an economy of the many. The automobile industry is an economy of the few
6.   (Generally) Stay with what you know, although there are notable exceptions
7.   **Cannot ultimately get away from replacement value vs. economic value**
8.   **Always....there will be surprises**
9.   Don't squeeze last nickel out of a project....buying or selling
10. Don't look back ("if only I had known")
11. Buy what you can afford to pay for
12. **If a construction job starts "sour", it will continue that way unless work is stopped**

TIPS

1.   Maintain continuity of projects "in the hopper"
2.   Cultivate relationships - contractors, lenders, brokers, designers, etc.
3.   10 year spread sheets are a nice computer exercise....that's about all!
4.   Be certain that all parties understand the timing for permit processing
5.   Hire an expert (feasibility, etc.) early on if you are inexperienced
6.   Get the local pulse if going into a new area

ON DOING SOMETHING
1.   Even if you are on the right track, you'll get run over if you just sit there.
     Will Rogers
2.   If you don't know where you're going, when you get there you'll be lost.
     "Yogi" Berra
3.   One day Alice came to a fork in the road and saw a Cheshire cat in a tree.
     "Which road do I take?" she asked.
     His response was a question: "Where do you want to go?"
     "I don't know," Alice answered.
     "Then," said the cat, "it doesn't matter."
     Lewis Carroll in Alice in Wonderland

FEASIBILITY

SITE EVALUATION AND RISK FACTORS

PROPERTY ACQUISITION CHECKLIST

PROPERTY ADDRESS/DESCRIPTION_____
Open Escrow Subject To: (a) approval of title report, (b) engineering studies,
(c) issuance of use [or building] permit; (d) marketing feasibility study, (e)
terms of payment, (f) date of occupancy, or (g) other?

SITE CHECKLIST

1.   Easements - overhead/underground
2.   Unrecorded easements; prescriptive rights?
3.   Required street frontage set back
4.   Bonded assessment, if any (recorded) NOTE: see Land Purchase Agreement p. 7 & 8
5.   Acreage fees - Public Works or Building Department
6.   Other fees: fire and school district; traffic signalization; parks
7.   Utility connections - unrecorded. NOTE: may be by statute and unknown to City/County agencies
8.   Leases - recorded or unrecorded
9.   Uncompacted fill on site?
10. Drainage or underground water. Note green areas in the summertime
11. Street improvements required, if any
12. Water supply; pressure adequate for fire sprinklers?
13. Electrical power available; Utility Co._____
14. Cable TV available or required for project?
15. Dedicated telephone circuits required? Fiber-optics? Integrated infrastructure?
16. Current Zoning:_____; Desired Zoning;_____
     Current Zoning permits:_____(the use of)_____
17. Parking code regulations
18. Lot split or subdivision map to be filed?
19. Is rail spur available (industrial use only)
20. TIMING FOR PERMIT PROCESS
21. Two or more lots - lot consolidation required?
22. Is adjacent property available for purchase? Required for project?

COST OF OFF-SITE IMPROVEMENTS

Engineering, Soils Report	Lot Split/Subdivision Map
Sewers	Street Lighting
Curbs, Gutters, Sidewalks	Streets
Development Fees (per above)	Gas Service
Water Mains, Hydrants	Sewer Fees
Acreage Fees	Demolition
Fill Ground	Drainage
Relocate / Underground Existing Power Poles	Install New Power Poles
Storm Drains	Other?

BUILDING PURCHASE

Structural Renovation	Building Systems
Physical Condition	Conversion of Use
Lease Review/New Leases/Estoppel Statement	Technical/Service Manuals
Personnel Transfer	What Personal Property to Stay
Commitments - Service Contracts	Income/Expense (tax statements)

FEASIBILITY ANALYSIS

A. PROPERTY ACQUISITION CHECKLIST

I. **LOCATION**

Address:_____

City:_____ A.P. No.:_____

County:_____ State:_____

II. **PROPERTY**

Area:_____ (Sq. Ft.) Dimensions:_____ Shape:_____

Frontage/Street:_____ Width:_____

Easements:_____ Rights-of-Way:_____

Trees/Landscaping:_____

Special Features:_____

_____

Existing Uses:_____

Existing Structures:_____ Demolition:_____

Utility   Connections

Water:_____ Fire Water:_____ Sewer:_____

Stormwater Drainage:_____ Gas:_____

Electricity:_____ Telephone:_____ TV Cable:_____

Additional Comments

_____

Adjacent   Properties

Owners: Uses:

1._____   1._____

2._____   2._____

3._____   3._____

Other Projects in the Area:_____

III. **BUILDING(S)**

Building Areas:_____ No. of Floors:_____ Dimensions:_____

Construction Drawings:_____ Date:_____

Leases:_____ Personnel:_____

Condition:_____ Service Contracts:_____

Bldg. Systems:_____

Personal Property:_____

Income:_____ Expenses:_____

Existing Uses

Ground Floor:_____ 2nd Floor:_____

3rd Floor +:_____

IV. **GENERAL PLAN OR SPECIFIC AREA PLAN**

Changes to Site or Area:_____

Urban Design Requirements:_____

Off-Site Infrastructure Requirements:_____

Community Facilities Requirements:_____

V. **ZONING**

Existing Zoning:_____

Category:_____ Uses By Right:_____

Special Permit Uses:_____

Front Setback:_____ Rear Setback:_____

Side Setbacks:_____ Parking Requirements:_____

Height Limitations:_____ FAR:_____

Timing:_____ Conditions:_____

Reasons for Action:_____

VI. **SUBDIVISION**

Lot Consolidation:_____ Minor Subdivision:_____

Major Subdivision:_____

Dedications, etc:_____

Covenants &/or Restrictions:_____

VII. **PERMITS & APPROVALS PROCESS**

1. Use Permit:_____

2. Zoning Approval:_____

3. Design Review:_____

4. Subdivision Approval:_____

5. CEQA/EIR:_____

6. Highway Dept./Curb Cuts:_____

7. Utility Connections:_____

8. Construction Permit:_____

VIII. **FEES**

1. Water:_____ 6. Special District_____

2. Sewer:_____ 7. Development_____

3. School District:_____ 8. Assessments:_____

4. Environmental Impact:_____ 9. Other:_____

5. Acreage:_____ 10. _____

IX.   COSTS

Special Reports

1. Topographic Survey_____   5._____

2. Soils:_____   6._____

3. Market Survey:_____   7._____

4. Traffic Study:_____   8._____

Site Preparation

1. Grading:_____   6. Utilities:_____

2. Drainage:_____   7._____

3. Streets/Paving:_____   8._____

4. Lighting:_____   9._____

5. Street Furniture:_____   10._____

INFORMATION SOURCES

City and/or County
1. Planning Department
2. Highway Department
3. Water District
4. Flood Control District

5. Building Department
6. Public Works Department
7. School District
8. Assessor's Office

Region and/or State
1. Environmental Protection
2. Fish & Wildlife

3. CALTRANS/Highway
4. Economic Development

Federal
1. Corps of Engineers
2. General Services

3. Interior/Parks & Recreation
4. FAA (flight path)

Private
1. Water Company
2. Gas & Electric Utility

3. Railroad Company
4. Waste Collection

B. LAND PURCHASE AGREEMENT

I.   OPENING OF ESCROW

1. Approval of Title Report:_____

2. Completion of Engineering Studies:_____

3. Available Reports:_____

4. Issuance of Building/Use Permit:_____

5. Market Feasibility Study:_____

6. Terms of Payment:_____

7. Date of Occupancy:_____

8. CC&Rs:_____

9._____

II.   **ELEMENTS OF PURCHASE AGREEMENT**

Location

Address:_____

City:_____ Apt. No:_____

County:_____ State:_____

Preliminary Title Report

Approval Time:_____ Time to Cure Defects:_____

Conditions

Permits:_____ Financing:_____

Feasibility:_____ Other:_____

Build-to-Suit/Name:_____ Use:_____

Assessments

Seller's Responsibilities/Fees:_____

Buyer's Responsibilities:_____

Costs

Title Insurance:_____ Closing:_____

Brokerage Commissions

Responsibility:_____ Percent:_____

Utilities/Improvements

Services to Site:_____ Connection Fees:_____

Purchase Price

Amount:_____ Terms:_____

Escrow

Closing:_____ Office:_____

Prorations

Property Taxes:_____ Rentals:_____

Insurance:_____ Other:_____

Parties to the Agreement

Seller:_____ Owner/Nominee:_____

Assignments:_____ Execution:_____

Schedule

Acceptance:_____ Execution:_____

Disclosure

Liens:_____ Probate:_____

Hazardous Waste:_____ Other:_____

FEASIBILITY

LAND PURCHASE AGREEMENT

LOCATION Describe all factors; address, assessor's parcel no., total area

PRELIMINARY TITLE REPORT Time to approve (or disapprove); time for seller to cure defects; (initially a PROPERTY PROFILE, most likely) (Lot book guarantee)

PARCEL MAP/ENGINEERING DATA Legal lot to be conveyed? Any topographic maps, soils reports, street improvement plans, site development studies, and other related data which seller may have to be provided to buyer at no additional cost. NOTE: the time to obtain these is at opening of escrow!

CONDITIONS Use and/or building permits, feasibility, financing, etc.
NOTE: Large corporate sellers do not want to see "financing" as a condition. **If a "build-to suit", specify name and intended use. DEFINE APPROXIMATE TIME FRAME**

ASSESSMENTS Clarify seller's responsibilities....specifically water and sewer (deferred) fees which do not "run with the land" and are not shown on a title report. Excluded are buyer's fees necessary to obtain the building permit.
NOTE: Insure that seller cannot put on additional fees for your account- i.e. a new business; or industrial park or subdivision where no assessment district exists

TITLE INSURANCE/CLOSING COSTS Specify who pays for what; usually consistent with County practice and custom. **NOTE: from San Luis Obispo County south, custom is for seller to pay both title insurance and documentary stamps.** So. California also has "escrow offices"

REAL ESTATE BROKERAGE COMMISSIONS If applicable, define who pays

UTILITIES/IMPROVEMENTS Developed site includes all utilities available at least to the property line. Service/connection fees by buyer. Verify that frontage improvements, if recently installed, have been approved and accepted by the appropriate jurisdiction

PURCHASE PRICE Terms thereof

ESCROW CLOSING Time to close after all conditions met...30 days?

ESCROW OFFICE Name/address of title company. Buyer's selection

PRORATIONS Property taxes, rentals, insurance, etc.

ASSIGNMENT Right to buyer

OWNERSHIP Name of new future (proposed) owner or nominee. Possibility of 1031 (Starker) exchange at no additional cost or liability to seller

TIME Date for seller's acceptance, after which offer is null and void

FEASIBILITY

LAND PURCHASE AGREEMENT (Continued)

SELLER'S EXECUTION Seller's signature required (as present owner) on use permit application, etc. **Executed in a timely manner and power of attorney if seller is planning to be away**

DISCLOSURE STATEMENTS Hazardous waste materials; other full disclosures ('86 law with additional requirements thereafter) **NOTE: More stringent for residential property generally**

PROPERTY IN PROBATE?

The site evaluation and property analysis usually starts the development process. From now on, lots of balls have to be kept juggled into the air.

LAND PURCHASE AGREEMENT - ADDITIONAL NOTES
1. Know <u>precise</u> property or building area. Can mean large dollars!
2. **TAKE NOTHING FOR GRANTED IN WRITING THE OFFER**
3. Do not rely on dollars per s.f. pricing, excepting only at the onset
4. Property history - toxic wastes?
5. (Special) Qualifications for potential lessees/users or uses
6. Approvals from Cal-Trans (eg. fronting on State Highway), Fish and Game, Corps of Engineers, or other non-local agencies
7. **BE SURE THAT SELLER UNDERSTANDS THE TIMING FOR PERMIT PROCESSING AND ANY ENVIRONMENTAL IMPACT REQUIREMENTS**

NO PROPERTY IS SACROSANCT FROM THIS "PROCESS"! ALWAYS FOLLOW THE STEPS...EVEN IF YOU ALREADY OWN THE PROPERTY. DO THESE TO KEEP ABREAST OF THE MARKET PLACE.

**** UNDERSTAND THAT SOME SITES MAY NOT BE ECONOMICALLY OR PHYSICALLY DEVELOPABLE

ASSIGNMENT: **Use the checklists and notes herein to inspect a parcel of property, no matter the size.**

<u>**FEASIBILITY**</u>

<u>**PROFORMA/FINAL COST ESTIMATES**</u>

LAND COST
Land Purchase Cost (net if credit for brokerage commission is applicable)
Title and Closing Costs
Property Taxes - for holding period (or in holding cost below)

ORGANIZATIONAL COST
Legal and Accounting; Partnership/Venture Agreement(s)

DESIGN COST - PRELIMINARY
Schematic/Preliminary Drawings (architectural/engineering)
Soils Report, Toxic Tests, etc.
Use Permit Fees
Other Consulting Fees

DESIGN/DEVELOPMENT COST - FINAL
Final Working Drawings
Project Management

CONSTRUCTION COST (see detailed breakdown)
Building Permit Fees
"Hard Cost" Items
Supervision/Overhead
Contingency; percentage depending upon complexity/scope of project.
        Generally applies <u>only</u> to construction cost
        Maybe: The <u>bigger</u> the project the <u>smaller</u> the % for
        contingency. **Look at raw numbers**

REAL ESTATE BROKERAGE COMMISSIONS(S)
For Leasing;   typically, a 5 year lease = 25% of first year's income; a 10
year lease = 35 to 40% of the first year's income

CONSTRUCTION FINANCING
Interest on Construction Loan
Loan Points
Interest computed <u>from the day funds dispersed by lender</u>
Interest during leasing "start-up"

HOLDING COST/PERMANENT FINANCING
Operating/Management Costs
Credit for Rental Income
Loan Points
Escrow/Title Costs <u>(short rate premium set up with construction loan)</u>
Example:
$1,000,000 construction loan; 10-1/2% - 8 month construction period
$300,000 applied to land purchase
One year "lease-up"

$300,000 x 10-1/2% x 8 months	$21,000
$700,000 x 10-1/2% x 8 months x 60%	29,400
(all of the money for slightly more than half of the time)	
$1,000,000 x 10-1/2% x 1 year ("holding" period)	<u>105,000</u>

TOTAL CONSTRUCTION INTEREST = $155,400

FEASIBILITY
DEVELOPMENT RULES OF THUMB

Approximate Order of Magnitude Costs and Prices for PRELIMINARY PROFORMA ANALYSIS and/or PROPERTY ACQUISITION. This is a frame of reference; a place to start. Cost basis is 1997
NOTE: Permit Entitlement Fees, Development Fees, and A&E Design fees are Excluded Except as noted.

R E S I D E N T I A L ($185,000-225,000 home prices)

Unimproved Land	= $20,000-30,000 per lot
Improvements/Infrastructure	= $20,000-25,000 per lot
Engineering Fees for Tentative map	= $2,000-3,000 per lot

NOTE: Clearly define scope of work required

Direct Building Cost (1,000-1,500 s.f.)	= $70-80 per s.f.

NOTE: Minimal landscaping and "upgrades", fencing?

A P A R T M E N T

Unimproved Land - "Affordable" Units	= $10,000 per unit
" " - Moderately Priced	= $15,000 per unit
" " - Upper End; Garden	= $25,000 per unit

NOTE: Apartment "experts" say <u>never</u> pay more than $25,000 regardless......

Improvements/Infrastructure	= Varies greatly
Direct Building Cost	= $80+ per s.f.(apartment size)

NOTE: Smaller the apt., higher the cost per s.f. due to utility and equipment load; i.e. kitchen, bathroom cost are the same whether a studio or 2BR unit

C O M M E R C I A L

Unimproved Land	= Varies; Market Income determines
Improvements/Infrastructure	= incl. Building Shell(s) below
Industrial - Building Shell (1)	= $30-35 per s.f.(all are building area)
Offices-Garden/Low Rise-Bldg.Shell(1)	= $55-60 per s.f. " " " "
Retail - Building Shell (1)	= $50-55+? per s.f." " " "
Tenant Improvements (TI's)	= $35-40+ per s.f. of <u>improved</u> area

NOTES:
a. Retail may have fixturization/improvements by tenant(s)
b. Building shell prices are for standard, non-hazardous occupancies
c. Wall to floor area ratios and floor area coverage/ratios (site coverage) are critical to cost. Above price ranges are for "standard or normal" projects.
(1) Building Shell includes site completed, "ready-to-go"; landscaped, paved etc., building exterior completed and "secure", ready for Tenant Improvements (TI's)

OPERATING EXPENSES
25-35% of Gross Income. Apartments tend to the lower percentage; offices to the higher percentage. San Jose luxury apartments = 28%-35%

ULI Land Use Digest 9, September 1994:
The apartment facility is costed out for a 6-story, 60,000 s.f building with 10'-4" story heights, face brick with concrete block back-up and a steel frame. Costs do not include site work, land costs, development cost, or specialty finishes or equipment.
Following is cost per sq. ft.:

	1996	1997	1998
San Francisco Metro Area	$108	$113	$112
Los Angeles Metro Area	$ 97	$100	$100
San Diego Metro Area	$ 94	$ 97	$ 97

FEASIBILITY

ECONOMIC ANALYSIS - LAND VALUE

Following is an actual study of a property which has multi-use zoning; retail _and_ residential (12-20 units per acre). The analysis is for the residential portion only and was used in conjunction with a similar analysis of the retail portion to confirm <u>appraised land valuations which turned out to be 18% ($300,000)</u> **high!**

Projected development, as approved: 14 apartment units; 0.93 acres = 40,511 sf
Rental Rates: $650 - 1BR (7 ea.); $800 - 2BR (7 ea.)

The Analysis:

	Minimum	**Maximum**
Annual Income - 14 units	$ 121,800	$ 121,800
Less 5% Vacancy	[6,090]	[6,090]

GROSS INCOME	**$ 115,710**	**$ 115,710**
Less Operating Expense: Taxes, Insurance, CAM, etc.	[34,710] (30%)	[28,930] (25%)

NET OPERATING INCOME	**$ 81,000**	**$ 86,780**
CAPITALIZED VALUE	**$ 900,000 (9%)**	**$1,084,700 (8%)**
LOAN AMOUNT -75%	**$ 675,000**	**$ 813,500**
Total Development Cost	$ 729,200	$ 729,200
RESIDUAL LAND VALUE	**$ 170,800**	**$ 355,500**
PER UNIT (14 units)	**12,200**	**25,400**
PER S.F. OF LAND (40, 511 sf)	**4.22**	**8.78**

NOTE: Brokerage commissions which may be due from any sale, <u>are not</u> deducted from the capitalized value.

<u>Economic Analysis - Loan Amount</u>

	Minimum	**Maximum**
Cost Value x 85% [Development Cost + Residual Land Value]	$ 765,000	$ 922,000
Economic Value x 75%	675,000	813,500
Debt Service Value - 1.15 (10%-25 yrs.)	**641,000***	**687,000***

* Controlling for loan amount

FEASIBILITY

DEVELOPMENT PROFORMA - CASE STUDY

(All figures rounded to nearest 100)

LAND COST		= $ 1,504,000
Land - 8 ac. =348,480 sf @ $4.25	= 1,481,000 (3)	
Title and Closing Costs	= 4,500	
Property Taxes; 12 mos. @ 1.25%	= 18,500	

ORGANIZATIONAL COSTS (Legal & Accounting)	=	5,000

PRELIMINARY DESIGN ANALYSIS		= 18,000
Schematic Drawings for Use Permits	= By Owner	
Soils Report	= 5,000	
Phase I - Environmental Assessment	= 2,000	
NO TOXIC TESTING INCLUDED		
Use Permit Fees	= 1,000	
Miscellaneous Consulting Fees	= 10,000	

FINAL DESIGN AND DEVELOPMENT COSTS		= 464,400
Final Working Drawings; Arch/Engr	= 125,000	
Building Permit/Plan Check [50% of building permit]	= 14,700	
Acreage/Development Fees **[3] [4]**	= 324,700	
[see summary detail following]		

BUILDING CONSTRUCTION COST		= 4,242,900
Office Shell: 30,000 sf @ $43.50	= 1,305,000	
Office TI's: 30,000 sf @ $25.00	= 750,000	
Garage/Shop Shell: 10.250 sf @ $27.50	= 281,900	
Garage/Shop TI's: 10,250 sf	= By Owner	
Closed Storage, Non-hazardous:		
4,700 sf @ $20.00	= 94,000	
Closed Storage, Hazardous: 2,400 sf @ $40	= 96,000	
Covered Storage, Open Sides:		
4,450 sf @ $10.00	= 44,500	
Fire Sprinklers: 47,350 sf @ $2.00	= 94,700	
Sitework: 3 ac. = 130,680 sf @ $3.50 **[1]**	= 457,400	
Sitework: 5 ac. = 217,800 sf @ $2.25 **[2]**	= 490,000	
NO OFFSITE STREET/UTILITY WORK		
Project Supervision: 12 mos. @ $5,000	= 60,000	
Contactor's OH&P **[no bond]** @ 10%	= 367,400	
Contingency - 5%	= 202,000	

REAL ESTATE BROKERAGE COMMISSIONS(S)	=	**None**

SUB TOTAL	=	**$6,234,300**

[1] Grading, Paving, Landscaping, Utilities, Curbs, Striping, etc.
[2] Grading, Paving, Some Utilities
[3] Depending upon property location
[4] Conservative; maximum for each jurisdiction used
    [see summary detail following]

FEASIBILITY

DEVELOPMENT PROFORMA (Continued)

SUB TOTAL (preceding page)   = $ 6,234,000

FINANCING COSTS [$6,000,000 loan: one year]   =   664,800
Points; Permanent/Const. - 3%   =   180,000
Escrow Fees; CLTA Short Rate   =   16,000
ALTA Premium   =   3,000
Lender Appraisal   =   5,000
Construction Interest: [Prime + 2%]
   Land: 600,000 x 12%   =   72,000
   Improvements: 5,400,000 x 12% x 60%   =   388,800

                        TOTAL DEVELOPMENT COST   = $ 6,899,100

                        PROBABLE LEASE RATE   = $758,900 TO 827,000
                        PER YEAR

                        [11-12% factor]   = $63,200 to 69,200
                        PER MONTH
                        NET-NET-NET LEASE

SCHEDULE OF DEVELOPMENT FEES (For example only- have been increased)

School & Fire Districts: $.50 per sf x 47,350   = $ 23,675 *
Sewer Connection [Napa County] $.72/sf x 47,350   =   34,092 *
  Probable "substantial" increase in near future
Sewer Connection [Amer. County] 85.56 per FU
  Min. = $1,711; say 30 FU @ 85.56   =   2,567
[Proposed] Recreation Fees [Amer. County]
  $875 = $438/employee; 2 "free"
  875 = 263 x 438   =   115,806 *
Traffic Impact Fee [Napa County] **Not yet enacted**
  "Guesstimate"; plus/minus 30%!!   =   100,000
Fire Connection [Amer. County]   =   4,531
Fire Connection [Napa City]; **no one seems to know**   =   ???
Plan Check - Fire [Amer. County]   =   1,000 *
  "   "   " [Calif. Forestry]   =   none
  "   "   " [Napa City] $62.39/hr   = no maximum; no estimate
Mitigation - Fire [Amer. Canyon]   =   9,309 *
  30,000 sf office = 4,929;
  20,000 sf industrial = 4,380
Water [Napa City]:1"= 1,320; 1 1/2" = 2,060; 2" =2,475 = 2,475
Water [Amer. Canyon] 1" = 11,327; 1 1/2" = 22,655 = 36,248 *
  2" = 36,248

NOTE: Items marked * total $324,661, and are the maximums noted for
    "Acreage/Development Fees"

FEASIBILITY

TYPICAL RANGE OF PRE-CONSTRUCTION FEES AND COSTS
Circa 1994; for reference only

Use Permit [typical, most agencies]	= $600-1,000 incl. Design Review

Concord has use permit fees to $1,600 for "unique or special circumstances"
plus design review fees of $200-800

Subdivision Map Fees [Contra Costa Co.]

Improvement Plan Check	= 2.5% x cost of improvements
Map Check Fee	= $700 + $30 per lot
Map Check Fee [Concord]	= $900 + $75 per lot + $800 Engineering
Phase I - Environmental Assessment	= $1,000 -2000
Lender's Appraisal	= $2,500+/-
Soils Report	= $3,500 [to $5,000?]
Toxic Studies [Phase II]	= $3,500+/- per boring plus report
A&E Drawings for Use Permit	= $2,000-5,000 [minimum range]
Engineering - Subdivision Maps	= $2,000+/- per lot

Other Permits/Fees [sample]

Fire and School District - Commercial	= $.50 per sf [typical Statewide]
Residential	= up to $10 per sf
Street Improvement [Concord]	= $3.33-5.07 per sf, commercial
	= $1,000 per unit, residential
Park Land, in lieu of dedication	= $726-1,608 per living unit [Concord]
Public Art [many places]	= 1/2% of cost; residential/commercial
Child Care [Concord]	= 1/2% of cost; commercial only
Drainage [Concord]	= up to $1,240 per acre
Drainage [Antioch]	= $.34 per sf impervious area
Traffic Signalization [Antioch]	= $.275 per s.f. of building
Recreation Fees [American Canyon]	= $875 + $438 per employee
Water Meter - 1"	= $410 [Antioch]
	= $1,320 [City of Napa]
	= $11,327 [Amer. Canyon Co.]
Water Meter - 1-1/2"	= $2,060 [City of Napa]
	= $22,655 [Amer. Canyon Co.]
Sewer Connection [commercial]	= $3,600 per 1" water meter [Antioch]
	= $.72 per sf [Napa County]
	= $85.56/FU [Amer. Canyon Co.]

Building Permit [per Uniform Building Code] plus 50-65% for Plan Check

$50-100,000	= $414.50 + $4.50 ea $1,000 over $50,000
$100,000-500,000	= $639.50 + $3.50 ea $1,000 over $100,000
$500,000-1,000,000	= $2,039.50 + $3.00 ea $1,000 over $1,000,000
Over $1,000,000	= $3,539.50 + $2.00 ea $1,000 over $1,000,000

NOTE: Many jurisdictions use the UBC table although large cities may have their own schedule. Concord is unusual for a city of its size and has a fee of 1/4%-2.5% of the cost. Many, if not most, jurisdictions have "standard" costs per s.f. for various building types which they use.

CATEGORIES AND DESCRIPTION OF CONSTRUCTION COSTS

PLANS - Architect/Engineer, Landscaping, Soils, Rendering, Mechanical,
    NOTE: HVAC, Plumbing, Electrical, Fire Sprinklers mostly
    by Contractor except on larger projects
LAND SURVEY/TOPOGRAPHY
PERMITS - Use Permit/Design Review, Plan Check/Building, Sewer and Water Fees,
    Sewer Assessment, Acreage/Drainage Fees, Traffic Signalization,
    School/Fire District, etc. etc.
DEMOLITION
SITE PREPARATION INCL. CONSTRUCTION STAKING - Clearing and grubbing,
    recompaction, stripping
GRADING & FILL/BUILDING PAD - Fine/rough grading, rock pad
STORM DRAINAGE - Catch basins; onsite/offsite connections
STRUCTURAL FOOTINGS - Concrete, piling, piers, etc.
STRUCTURAL FLOOR - Concrete, [mesh/rebar], wood frame
STRUCTURAL WALLS - Concrete, wood, masonry, steel, etc.
CONCRETE WALKS - Sidewalks, brick pavers
CONCRETE DRIVEWAYS/APRONS
MISCELLANEOUS CONCRETE - Curbs, planters, architectural features
WOOD FRAMING - EXTERIOR
STRUCTURAL ROOF SYSTEM
ROOFING - Composition [hot mop], tile, shingles/shakes, etc.
ASPHALT PAVING - Fine grading, rock base, field testing for thickness
LANDSCAPING/IRRIGATION
BUMPER GUARDS/STRIPING - Parking areas....HDCP requirements
STRUCTURAL STEEL/ARCHITECTURAL METAL/ORNAMENTAL IRONWORK
FENCING - Concrete, Masonry, Chain Link.....trash enclosures
ARCHITECTURAL MASONRY - incl. Plaster
INSULATION - Foil, batts, spray-on, etc.
EXTERIOR DOORS - Truck doors, HM man doors, entries, incl. hardware
GLASS & GLAZING/STOREFRONTS - incl. mirrors
SKYLIGHTS
PAINTING - Exterior and interior [segregate]
PLUMBING - Rough and finish; segregate for payments. Connection fees
ELECTRICAL - Rough and Finish; segregate for payments
HEATING & AIR COND. - Roof/bathroom vents, sheet metal flashing,downspouts, etc.
INTERIOR FRAMING - Wood/steel studs, joists
INTERIOR DRYWALL - Walls and ceilings; acoustical ceiling
FIRE SPRINKLERS - Onsite hydrant/ incl. connections
INTERIOR WOOD/METAL DOORS - incl. hardware
SPECIAL FINISHES/CABINETRY/WALLPAPER
BATHROOM FINISHES - Toilet partitions, ceramic tile/marlite wainscote,
    HDCP bars/signs
FLOORING - Carpet, vinyl comp. tile, marbelized tile, etc.
BUILDING SIGNAGE/DIRECTORY
TEMPORARY FACILITIES/UTILITIES, JOB CLEAN-UP, CONSTRUCTION
INSURANCE
CONTINGENCY/SUPERVISION

FEASIBILITY

MARKET RESERCH AND MARKETABILITY

GENERAL Which comes first, economic or market/marketability analyses? In other words, do [economic] feasibility studies emanate from market analyses or vice versa. If building and development costs are fairly well established or known, then market analyses would come first to determine if the project is viable. If the market <u>appears</u> to support a proposed project and costs are uncertain, then the feasibility study would come first. As a developer gains more and more experience, especially with repetitions of a specific type of product, feasibility and market analyses are performed concurrently. We will begin here with the [economic] feasibility analysis.

PRELIMINARY STEPS TO MARKET AND ECONOMIC STUDIES:

FIRST Obtain a general feel for the market in the area: activity, inventory/absorption, prices for the land and buildings, availability, broker/lender/contractor signs on properties, etc. **KNOW THE AREA. DO LOTS OF DRIVING AROUND.**

SECOND Obtain the services of a trusted consultant....developer, broker, engineer, architect, etc. ... for technical assistance in areas outside of your experience "comfort zone". This just may be the <u>best</u> money you will spend.

THIRD What is the market for your product?
1. Isolate the competition; Hayward example: 4 million sf. vacant, yet <u>competing</u> with only 150,000 s.f.
2. Sources for market analyses: local colleges [Cal State-Hayward, St. Mary's], and City/County/ABAG projections among many others. NOTE: Unfortunately, many expensive "market research" studies usually are not very valuable or reliable. And, they may be required by a lender!
3. **Market KNOWLEDGE, not market ANALYSIS** [eg.- So. California developer sent son to live in Orange County from L.A. for a year to do <u>nothing</u> else except gain knowledge about the marketplace]
4. May have to determine marketing data where no raw data presently exists.
5. Notwithstanding the foregoing, you still may have a "gut feeling" as to the development potential.

FOURTH Mapping
1. Locate your competition
2. Driving time [concentric circles] which may be different from actual mileage
3. Traffic and congestion....hours of the day
4. Access to principal roadways and freeways. Full or partial access?
5. "Barriers": physical, as in bridges; emotional, as in change for phone area code, different County, etc.
6. Footnote for property costs, rental rates, and other pertinent data

FIFTH   Facts in Community Profile

Utility Availability	Other Services [eg. snow plowing]
Business/Political Climate	Community Characteristics/Attitudes
Restaurants/Shopping	Churches and Hospitals
Local Taxes	Parks/Recreational/Cultural
Crime; Police and Security	Trash/Waste; esp. for Restaurants

FEASIBILITY

MARKET RESEARCH AND MARKETABILITY [continued]

How to collect data when there is no data to collect
Remember to have market knowledge, not market analysis.

CANNOT DELEGATE RISK AND DO NOT LACK IMAGINATIVE AUDACITY!
Researchers are often irresponsible about their findings in that they do not explain adequately what the findings mean and how the entity hiring/doing the research may improve its position by making use of the findings. Mediocre reports often are presented because researchers do not want to present what they cannot verify readily with statistics. Methods which rely on complete documentation can be the organization's worst enemy when it comes to attaining market leadership, **because such data may not exist.....it must be invented!** Expert analysts sometimes make recommendations which go beyond data. It takes the broad understanding of a real expert to see what makes sense even where there is not enough information to make this obvious.

FORECASTS ARE OFTEN PROJECTIONS OF WHAT HAS HAPPENED ALREADY. A manager may become committed emotionally to non-stop growth (i.e. building) when he is intellectually aware that his industry is cyclic and that substantial risks are associated with failure to take this cyclic nature into account.

The foregoing and following are courtesy of: Steve D. Ugbah, PhD
                    Professor-Dept.of Marketing
                    School of Business and Economics
                    California State University at Hayward

MARKETING RESEARCH
The systematic gathering, recording, and analyzing of data about problems relating to the marketing of products to guide clients or yourself. A formal communication link with the environment, community, etc.

PURPOSE: to provide accurate and useful information; specifying, collecting, analyzing and interpreting for planning, problem solving and control for better decision making.

STEPS
1. Define problem and identify objectives. **Distinguish between problem and symptom. Symptom: property not leasing; Problem: rate too high**
2. Determine research design [process]
3. Determine method of data collection
4. Design data collection forms
5. Design the sample and collect data within the constraints of cost, time and resources
6. Process, analyze and interpret data
   NOTE: these first six items can be deadly dull. Try to enliven them!
7. Prepare research report with condensed, concise information
8. Communicate findings....for self or client
   NOTE: the last two are exciting! and the meat of the work and effort

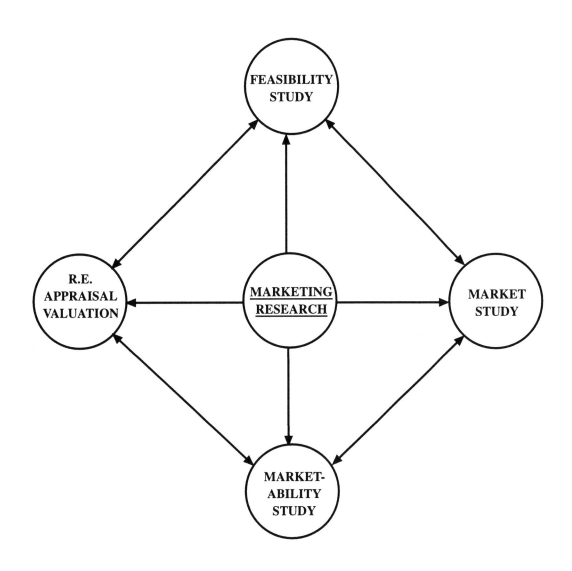

Common Thread for all of these: DATA or INFORMATION

MARKET RESEARCH———————►ENVIRONMENT————————►INFORMATION———————————►BETTER DECISIONS

[situation]
[phenomena]

M A R K E T   R E S E A R C H   F O R   R E A L   E S T A T E
P R O J E C T S

Courtesy of: **Steve D. Ugbah, PhD**
Professor - Dept. of Marketing
School of Business and Economics
California State University at Hayward

- 19 -

FEASIBILITY

MARKET RESEARCH AND MARKETABILITY [continued]

RESEARCH OBJECTIVE #1   Determine the number of students at Cal State-Hayward holding part-time or full time jobs during the school year. **Manageable?**
RESEARCH OBJECTIVE #2   Determine the impact which holding an outside job has on a student's academic performance. **Probably not manageable**
RESEARCH OBJECTIVE #3 Assess the value of holding a job while attending college **Not Manageable**

RESEARCH DESIGNS [Present Results to Clients]
1. Exploratory - preliminary; limited information. NO CONCLUSIVE STATEMENTS
2. Descriptive - ask more pointed questions. Better appreciation of problem
3. Casual [experimental] - controlled data

EXAMPLE - MARKETING RESEARCH STUDY IN ANTIOCH [Cal State-Hayward]
1. Light Industrial; "no-go", but triggered more questions to ask and analyze
2. Limited initial response due to contact during business work hours
3. Ethics in disclosing names of prospects
4. Auto Centre; consumer study and contacted at home. Higher initial response
5. Worked very closely with researchers [students]
6. Clearly defined [a] computer printout data, and [b] what questions asked

DEFINITION OF TERMS
Market Study   The comparison of market analysis projections with the supply of space for a specified activity in an attempt to identify market opportunities

Market Analysis A dynamic process involving the projections with the supply of the components of demand

Economic Base Study An analysis of the employment and income-generating activities in an economically or geograhically defined area

Marketability Study   Determines to what extent a particular piece of property can be marketed under various development concepts; more generally, determines the ability of a market to absorb space within a specific use or time. Does not involve the consideration of the development costs or profitability.

Strategy Study Determines the best location and marketing advantages for entrance into new, unexplored market areas, such as retail chains

Volume Expectancy Study   Determines total sales volume for department store trade merchandise and comparison goods at shopping centers - [demographics, daytime employment reports, trade area maps, site specific marketing maps, etc.].

Feasibility Study Includes the economic proforma. Determines whether a project is a "go" or "no-go" situation at a specific site, given certain financial criteria

Highest and Best Use Study Determines which physically or reasonably possible, appropriately supportive, financially feasible, and legally permissable use results in the highest land [development] value. Not a marketability study. Maybe best for "infill" projects?

FEASIBILITY

MARKET RESEARCH AND MARKETABILITY [continued]

OVERVIEW SUMMARY AND COMMENTS

THE EXPERTS "Experts", in making economic forecasts, seem to be "right" 50%of the time. We never hear about the times when they were "wrong"....there is some technical term for it as "market correction". For example, prominent California banks and many national financial advisors forecast [a] much higher mortgage rates, and [b] double digit inflation for 1989. Through the first half of 1989, interest rates dropped and inflation was no worse than medium, single digit 1988 levels. If one preaches "famine and pestilence" forever, ultimately there will be a period when they are "right". We can all be "expert" by paying strict attention to our own marketplace, continually looking at our own intuition, and staying within our established niche and "comfort zone." This same scenario occurred in the early '90s under slighty different criteria.

TIMING As discussed previously, the development industry is a business of the many, not the few; hence there are many, many outside and uncontrollable factors. Timing, for development, is probably [a] more an art than a science, and [b] greatly aided by the "experience curve"

TERMINOLOGY "Market" and "marketability" studies are commonly, in error, referred to as "feasibility" studies

LARGE AND SMALL PROJECTS Both smaller and large scale projects can fail for the same reason.....**lack of proper market analysis.** Small-scale developments require the same general framework of market analysis as large-scale developments

APPRAISALS Institutional lenders have asked for an "appraisal" for a construction loan when, in fact, a feasibility study would be more suitable for their purpose, and in the mid '90s they were beginning to ask for such

PROPERLY CONDUCTED MARKET ANALYSIS Can achieve the following: [1] Identify market opportunity, that is market shortages in the entire market area or locational deficiencies in specific sectors of the marketing area, [2] aid in the design and implementation of marketing strategies and plans, [3] serve as a guide in formulating development proposals for new properties or improved properties where conversions/renovation are being considered, and [4] establish rent or value levels

THE BAD NEWS Given that you have experience and a prudent and properly executed marketing/marketability/feasibility study, funds may be unavailable through conventional lending sources and the "great idea" may lie fallow for a period of time until institutions make a break with tradition. The list of project types which, initially, were very difficult to finance and now are accepted readily, include residential condominia and town homes, office condominia, public mini-storage, and recreational vehicle storage projects

DIRECT MAIL LIKELY RESPONSES [100=best]
Jan. = 100; Feb. = 95; Mar. = 90
Apr. = 75; May = 70; June = 65
July = 60; Aug. = 85; Sept. = 75
Oct. = 90; Nov. = 80; Dec. = 70

DATA ACCURACY FOR PROJECT TYPE
1.   RETAIL [shopping centers]
2.   HOUSING
2A.   APARTMENTS
3.   INDUSTRIAL
4.   OFFICES

FEASIBILITY

MARKET RESEARCH AND MARKETABILITY (Continued)

THE MARKET PLACE

Demographics

Chamber[s] of Commerce

Disposable Income, Age, etc.

Market Research Firm

State Sales Tax Data by Zip Code

Planning Agency General Plans

Economic Sources

Competition; Price/Location

Mapping Techniques

Project Signs (Bank, Broker, etc.)

Market Segmentation

Do Lots of Driving Around

Current Absorption/Inventory

The major commercial brokerage houses publish this information (by product type) on a frequently updated basis. Insure that data contains **net absorption** figures. For Bay Area residential activity: local Board of Realtors, Building Association of No. California, Anthony Hurt and Associates, Dataquick

Market Rates; For Sale or Lease

Also included in "Mapping" and "Absorption/Inventory". Is there a real opportunity for condominia (residential or commercial) sales?

Depth, Breadth, and Seasoning of the Market

How solid and strong is the market? How new is it?

User Profile

What are the motivations and requirements of the ultimate end user? What services and amenities need to be provided?

The Market Place

Very difficult to quantify. "protect the downside and the upside......anticipating the worst....can run free. If you plan for the worst - if you can live with the worst.....the good will always take care of itself." ("The Art of the Deal", Donald Trump)

Marketing Plan Implementations

Who sets up the plan and who runs it? How is it administered? Reporting?

Community Profile/Attitude

Growth/No Growth

Safety/Security

Parks and Recreation

Restaurants, Shopping

Public Transportation

Colleges, Universities

Cultural/Blue Collar

Financial or Distribution Center

Convention/Tourism

Schools, Churches, Hospitals

Postal Service, UPS, Federal Express

And More....

Financeable?

Everything looks great! Is the project financeable, or is it as mini-storage and condominia were several years ago?

FEASIBILITY

BROKERAGE/MARKETING IN PROJECT SUPPORT

References:
California Department of Real Estate, REFERENCE BOOK; published by State of California, Department of Real Estate, 1980
INDUSTRIAL REAL ESTATE, 4th Edition, published by Society of Industrial Realtors, Education Fund, Washington, DC, 1984

PRE-PROJECT DESIGN AND MARKETING CONSULTATION

MARKET DESIGN
Existing Market Base/Segmentation by Types
Existing Inventory by Types
Past Absorption History
Transportation
Labor Supply - Productivity

Government Climate
Business Cycles
Industry Economic Change[s]
Raw Material

SITE ANALYSIS
Location
Access
Use Restrictions
Physical Attributes
NOTE: Brokers want fast response time from developers, too -especially for proposals & "build-to-suits"

BUILDING FEATURES
Office Buildout [tenant improvements]
Available Power
Ceiling Height
Doors: Grade-Level vs. Dock-High [industrial only]
Parking
Rail Service [industrial only]
Bay Sizes [clear spans]
Type of Construction
Adaptability of Space

PROJECT MARKETING PLAN

SIGNING

PROJECT LITERATURE
Brochures
Flyers
Availability/Units/Pricing

INDIRECT COMMUNICATIONS
Public Relations
Broker Mailings/Open Houses/"Specials"
Target Tenants
Target Tenant Groups
Advertising

FEASIBILITY

BROKERAGE/MARKETING IN PROJECT SUPPORT [continued]

PROJECT MARKETING PLAN [continued]

DIRECT COMMUNICATION
Internal Brokers
External Brokers
Institutional
Potential Tenants
Target Geographical Areas

FOLLOW-UP AND ADMINISTRATION

COMPETITIVE ANALYSIS

REPORTING [Potential Tenants, Deals, Lost Deals, etc.]

LEASE/SALE NEGOTIATIONS

WHY USE A BROKER?

Accountability
Time [Economies of Scale]
Market Knowledge
Credibility
Objectivity In And Of Negotiations
Do You Hire Other Professionals?
Paid Only On Performance

SELECTING A BROKER

Referrals
Market Knowledge/Experience
Look To The Individual
Professional Affiliations - Broker vs. Agent
Understand Broker Compensation And Listing Agreement
Hire An Objective Advocate
Get A Time Commitment
Be Cautious Of Conflicts Of Interest
Personal Compatability

This applies to market research and brokerage project support:

"A wise man will make more opportunities than he finds" - **Francis Bacon**

<u>BROKERAGE/MARKETING IN PROJECT SUPPORT</u> [continued]

<u>HOW TO AVOID PROBLEM AREAS</u>

SET CLEAR WRITTEN POLICIES
Pricing
Commissions
  Percentage to be paid
  Exclusions [Net vs. Gross]
  When Paid
  Paid on Lease Extensions or Options?
  Area Customs/Competition
  Renewals

ESTABLISH JOINT RESPONSIBILITIES AND PRIORITIES ON MARKETING EFFORTS

BE CAREFUL OF PROCURING CAUSE
Set a Client Registration Policy
Be Consistent

PROCURING CAUSE   That cause originating from a series of events that, without break in continuity, results in the prime object of an agent's employment producing a final buyer [or lessee];   <u>the real estate agent who first procures (brings not tells) ready, willing, and able buyer [or lessee] for the agreed upon price and terms and is entitled to the commission</u>

EDITORIAL COMMENT   Real Estate brokers are the life blood of the development industry, and alienating them from your project[s] reduces by a significant number the amount of prospects which you will see. A good broker more than earns their commission. And <u>anything</u> which you pay a bad broker is too much!
[Mark Noe]

Assignment: Meet or talk with a real estate broker or developer

FEASIBILITY

THE PERMIT PROCESS

Entitlements To Use
Most Important: Understand the total process and procedures, and know what questions to ask

The Role of Local Government in Real Estate Development
Prepare and maintain long range plans and policies
Has "police power"
Review and process development applications
  Zoning Administrator [usually senior staff member]
  Design Review Commission [professional panel appointed]
  Planning Commission [lay panel appointed]
  City Council/Board of Supervisors [elected]
  NOTE: Planning Staff usually has no vote, makes recommendations; but in some jurisdictions, the
         local ordinance can delegate approval/denial authority to staff person with appeal provisions

Planning Regulations Affecting Real Estate Development
California Environmental Quality Act [CEQA]
Subdivision Map Act
  Specific requirements for denial
  Certain rights for subdivisions
  Vesting Map; approved for a longer period of time; usually approve all items
Permit Streamlining Act
Hazardous Waste Management Plan
General Plan
  General Plan, Specific Plan and Zoning are legislative acts
  Compelling cause to amend. No right to amend

Single Family Development
Zoning
Design Review [when applicable]
Variances
  Relatively minor conditions
  Unique to your property; not for all properties
  For conditions relating to property only
Building Codes/Fire Codes/Utility Requirements
Dedications and Exactions

Commercial Developments, Subdivisions, Apartments [usually]
Zoning [a requirement, not a suggestion]
Public Agency Referral
CEQA Requirements
*Design Review
*Planning Commission
Building Codes/Fire Codes/Utility Requirements
Dedications and Exactions
Use Permit generally required

* Some agencies allow hearings during EIR preparation if EIR required; risky!

FEASIBILITY
THE PERMIT PROCESS [continued]

LEAD AGENCY - responsible for all processing
RESPONSIBLE AGENCY - responsible for specific item of approval; eg. LAFCO with annexations;
  Fish & Game or Corps of Engineers with waterways

General Techniques to Improve processing
Research zoning including General Plan designation[s] and Specific Plans, if any
Obtain all necessary zoning maps, ordinances, etc. Also, information list for development projects which
  City/County must process under GC 65940, Permit Streamlining Act
Understand City/County procedures
Have site history well in mind
Know batting average of Planning Staff with Planning Commission/Council
  Who are proficient architects/engineers with approval "track record"?
  Ask about projects recently approved. Staff cannot "recommend" these consultants
Consider meeting with staff, neighborhood groups, and political leaders early in the process [possible
  negative impact from this is an early mobilization against project]
Use study sessions and field trips whenever possible
Effectively manage the process
  NOTE: Biggest gripe from planning staffs is "dealing with amateurs"
Make effective public presentations; attorney as presenter?
Development Agreement with agency [larger projects only] or rely on Vesting Tentative Map if
  applicable

Tips for the Process
Make your first appointment with the highest person with whom you can meet.
  **NOTE: For all but the most routine project, don't rely on over the counter or telephone
  information**
Come into initial meeting as prepared as possible
  Introduction from official in your city (if possible) if out of area
Attend "sample" commission meeting
  Hire local consultant if out of your area?
  Direct contact with commissioner[s] may be inappropriate. Find out
Determine timing for hearing[s]. Concurrent filing for use and/or zoning?
Fire District approvals required; cooperate with lead agency?
HDCP approvals, especially in renovations. Who interprets and how flexible are they?
Obtain feel for staff's [probable] recommendation/requirements ASAP!
Agency's policy or philosophy. High or low end of zoning range?
Follow filing instructions exactly [e.g. Antioch and Dublin]
Carefully monitor [weekly?] comments from responsible agencies during the 30 day review period
  following application
Hire outside [building permit] plan checker, if allowed, and there is a logjam
Keep abreast if out of your area - i.e. elections, moratoriums, etc.; use local newspapers, clipping services,
  phone book
Review of CC&R's [if required]. Crib from already approved CC&R's?

Environmental Impact Reports
Negative Declaration and/or Mitigated Negative Declaration
Focused EIR - 3 or 4 specific items such as traffic, noise, etc.
Full EIR - probably $15,000 minimum cost and 6 month's preparation time....while the project goes
  nowhere...plus certification time by commission[s]
Consultation with a knowledgeable land use attorney will be a good investment
Risky to proceed with design details while EIR is being processed

FEASIBILITY

THE PERMIT PROCESS [continued]

General

1.   Virtually all "horror stories" which I have heard re: permit processing omit pertinent   facts about the situation. However, "first hand" examples are:

    a. Purchase of $200,000 unimproved lot; did not know whether city or county
    b. Purchase of $2,900,000 building in Berkeley without checking anything with City

2.   City staffs tend to be more helpful [and knowledgeable?] than County staffs
    especially in smaller cities trying to make a "name"

Questions to Ask [although really an endless list!]

1.   What is General Plan designation; what does General Plan text say? Is there an applicable Specific Plan?
2.   What is actual, existing zoning? Conforms to General Plan?
3.   If not in conformance with General Plan, timeframe for rezoning? Will agency initiate rezoning?
4.   For #3, any likely opposition
5.   Is use permit required? [virtual certainty for income producing properties]
6.   May use permit include all projected, anticipated uses?
7.   Design review required? [virtual certainty except for one house/one lot]
8.   When do commissions meet?
9.   What is time to get on the agenda?
10.   What are application fees?
11.   Ordinances outside of zoning which apply; i.e. grading, trees, etc.?
12.   Will property dedications [eg. street widening] be required? What are Impact Fees, if any?
13.   Drought resistant planting? Mounded berms/lawns?
14.   Timing for subdivision approval? [details vary from agency to agency]
15.   Bonding of improvements required for Final Map?
16.   Installation of sidewalks or other frontage improvements?
17.   Are existing overhead utilities to be re-installed underground?
18.   Is a soils report required?
19.   What are acreage, utility connection, and other development fees?
    BE SURE TO CHECK WITH FIRE DISTRICT...may be collected seperately
20.   If fronting on a State Highway, will Cal-Trans allow curb cuts?
21.   Requirements for non-hazardous waste certification of property, even though there appears to be no evidence of toxics present?

ASSIGNMENT: Meet or talk with governmental planning person

USE PERMIT PROCESS

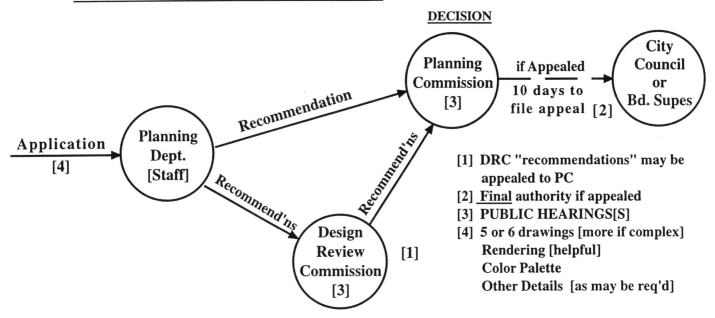

DECISION

Application [4] → Planning Dept. [Staff]

Recommendation → Planning Commission [3]

if Appealed
10 days to
file appeal [2] → City Council or Bd. Supes

Recommend'ns → Design Review Commission [3] [1]

Recommend'ns → Planning Commission [3]

[1] DRC "recommendations" may be appealed to PC
[2] _Final_ authority if appealed
[3] PUBLIC HEARINGS[S]
[4] 5 or 6 drawings [more if complex]
   Rendering [helpful]
   Color Palette
   Other Details [as may be req'd]

SUBDIVISION MAP PROCESS
Major Subdivisions - 5 or more lots

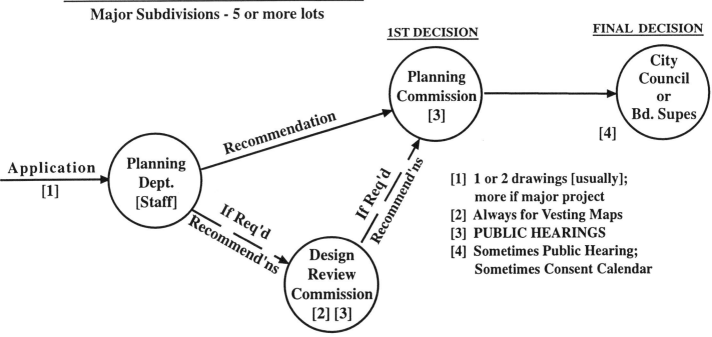

1ST DECISION   **FINAL DECISION**

Application [1] → Planning Dept. [Staff]

Recommendation → Planning Commission [3] → City Council or Bd. Supes [4]

If Req'd Recommend'ns → Design Review Commission [2] [3]

If Req'd Recommend'ns → Planning Commission [3]

[1] 1 or 2 drawings [usually]; more if major project
[2] Always for Vesting Maps
[3] PUBLIC HEARINGS
[4] Sometimes Public Hearing; Sometimes Consent Calendar

Identical Process for Tentative Map _and_ Final Map

C A S E   S T U D Y

"THE LABYRINTH OF PERMIT PROCESSING"

The subject case study is for an application to construct a church on property zoned R-20 [20,000 s.f. minimum lot size]. Churches are permitted uses in this zone, subject to the granting of a use permit. The project was controversial due to [a] traffic from 600 seat, 2-service utilization on Sunday, [b] substantial week night use for adult education classes, and [c] a lengthy and hardfought approval for a fundamentalist church within a half-mile distance of the property.

DAY ONE - ACQUIRED PROPERTY

Closed escrow for 5-1/2 acres. Prior meetings with Asst. Planning Director provided preliminary support from staff for the project's operation and function.

MONTH 3 - APPLICATION FOR USE PERMIT SUBMITTED

Initial staff recommendation was for a negative declaration. Notified on 28th day [of the 30 days required for application to be complete as submitted] that a Focused EIR would be required. Issues to be addressed were: [a] traffic, [b] noise from adjacent freeway, [c] hydrology [runoff], and [d] archaeological studies [possible Indian burial grounds]. These were to be the only issues to be addressed.

MONTH 4 - APPLICATION ACCEPTED; SUBJECT TO PREPARATION OF A FULL EIR

Political pressures from a well organized and effective local community action group caused Staff to expand the requirement to a full EIR. Met with Staff on the 30th day for this determination after previously written notification for a focused EIR. Met with Planning Director and Asst. Planning Director who each assured that permit would be approved if we followed their recommended procedures.

MONTH 5 - BEGAN EIR PROCESS

Meetings with the local community action group leaders. Several questions to answer regarding use of property by church. "Selected" EIR consultant; on roster of agency list, but really selected by applicant.

MONTH 6 - ACQUIRED ADDITIONAL PROPERTY

Bought 0.75 acres of "rock outcropping" property to preserve integrity of property, scenic views, etc., and to satisfy Parks District.

MONTH 13 - DRAFT EIR COMPLETED

During this period continued dialogue with community action group (several meetings) and made minor site plan and drawing revisions.

MONTH 16 - FINAL EIR COMPLETED

Cost was $13,500 and paid at the start of the process [month 5].

MONTH 17 - PUBLIC HEARING[S] SCHEDULED

90 day time extension requested by Staff and accepted by Applicant as the one year statute was about to run out. Public hearing rescheduled due to holidays and planning staff backlog. Public hearings to be held for [a] certification of the EIR, and [b] granting of the use permit. Staff continued to state that they would recommend approval of project, subject to "usual" conditions, none of which were onerous.

MONTH 18 - PUBLIC HEARINGS BEGAN

1st hearing was disjointed and unfocused due to Staff's inability to segregate the issues of first certifying [or rejecting] the EIR; secondly to discuss the use permit itself. 2nd hearing had procedural miscues in EIR consultant's lack of response to one letter [which letter was short and spoke of nothing new]....which, in reality, was not a miscue as the response was included in the EIR document, but neither staff nor consultant were aware of it! By the time applicant found the referenced document, the Commission had moved to another agenda item. [Applicant only remembered the document as the writer had an unusual last name.]

CASE STUDY [continued]

MONTH 20 - FINAL PUBLIC HEARING

Time running out on 90 day extension which was the last legal extension which could be made. Four [4] days prior to the hearing Staff casually informed applicant that they would be recommending denial of the project for vague reasons of design and impaction of the property. Choices were [a] proceed with hearing which would most likely have received a negative vote from the Planning Commission, [b] obtain a denial without prejudice, or [c] withdraw the application. Applicant opted to withdraw the application which allowed for faster [and less emotional] future processing time.

MONTH 21 - PROJECT REVISIONS

Met with Staff to resolve [a] design considerations and [b] utilization and use intensity of the property - especially a retail book store which was a non-permitted use in this zone. With the minor changes to be made, Staff could/would recommend approval of the project and certification of the EIR. 75% of the original filing fee was refunded, prompted by Applicant's threatened legal action and Staff's admission of their own culpability in the matter.

MONTH 22 - PROJECT ABANDONED

Congregation, tired of the processing rigors and confusion, withdrew much of their financial support, and determined to put the property up for sale. Total processing cost to date was $50,000 for EIR, architectural, engineering, and consulting fees plus approximately $66,000 in carry-back interest to Seller.

MONTH 38 - PROPERTY SOLD

New buyer closed escrow with certified EIR and plans for an 8-unit residential subdivision. To date [more than eight years later] no development of the property has occurred. The property was sold by the church for slightly less than its total initial investment [land cost, application processing costs, and interest carry-back to Seller].

HINDSIGHT FOR REDOING THE PROJECT

1. Have property purchase subject to granting of the use permit, a condition which probably was not acceptable to seller, and would have been more expensive as an option to purchase....but less overall [financial] exposure and internal chaos within the applicant's congregation.

2. Total "hands-off" selection of the consultant to prepare the EIR. The consultant made several procedural errors in preparation of the report, and Staff was always quick to point out that the consulting firm was not "their" selection.

3. From [1] above, the property [probably] would not have been purchased with an option and/or use permit conditions. Would have forced applicant's congregation to analyze seriously other alternatives.

4. More direct, "hands-on" involvement by the leadership of applicant's congregation. The cardinal rule of participation was violated.

What would YOU do differently?

FEASIBILITY

FINANCE PRINCIPLES

SOURCES OF MONEY:
Banks - multiple branches throughout State
Banks - local or regional branches only. Best source for "smaller loans". Know local market and borrower: can make a business loan, yet call it a real estate loan
Savings & Loans - consolidated; mostly single family residential and apartments
Individual Investors
Syndications - less prominent than in years past due to tax law changes
Insurance Companies/Pension Funds - rarely for loans under $10,000,000
Offshore Funds - currently (1998) very, very limited; "trophy buildings", completed projects, generally in urban areas
Mezzanine Lenders - lenders of equity who record a 2nd DT. Deeds may look and feel more like equity than debt

DEFINITIONS:
ORE/REO - Real Estate Owned [by Lender]. Foreclosed property
Mortgagor - a person who mortgages property; the borrower
Mortgagee - a person to whom property is mortgaged; the lender
DSR or DSC - Debt Service Coverage Ratio. The ratio of computed net income available to pay the principal and interest. Can range from 1.10 to 1.30 or higher
LTV - Loan to [appraised or economic] Value; usually the loan is 70-75% of the value
LTC - Loan to Cost - usually 80-90% of cost
Wraparound ["Wrap"] Mortgage - encompasses existing financing. May or may not be of record to the original lender. Possibility for foreclosure without "standard" procedures. Carry back by seller of the property. Face amount of the "wrap note" includes the equity of the lender [or seller] plus the underlying loan
Bullet Loan (Interim or Mini-Perm Loan) - as in "bite the bullet". Permanent loan with a short [3-5 year] due date. Sometimes used to describe "uncovered" construction loan
Subject To's - conditions which are "subject to" the original loan which is being assumed
Contract of Sale - seldom used anymore; not recorded, no formal title transfer
Hard Money Loan - for B or C credit and/or a difficult project, typically at very expensive terms. Term may have originated as hard to get

PERSPECTIVE OF THE LENDER:
Upside Potential - none
Downside Exposure - unlimited, particularly with toxic waste exposures
Profit - only from spread of cost of money

LENDING PHILOSOPHY:
Borrower, Credit, Real Estate
Real Estate, Credit, Borrower
Transaction vs. Relationship Oriented - the large developers have different borrowing terms than the rest of us!

LENDER SIZE AND SPECIALTY:
The right institution for the borrower and the project. Brokers are useful in this regard

LOAN ADMINISTRATION:
Documentation - may be documented in-house or by outside counsel
Disbursements - separate checks; wire transfers, or direct deposits; lien releases; sometimes made without retention until last draw

CREDIT AND THE "GOLDEN RULE"
Credit analysis in the conventional form. He who has the gold, rules!

FINANCE PRINCIPLES [continued]

WORKSHEET - ANALYZING THE INCOME PRODUCING PROJECT:

COST/PROJECT BUDGET
Hard Costs
Land [area x $_____ per s.f.] $_____
Site Development Cost   _____
Off-Site Development Cost   _____
Building Shell [area x $_____ per s.f.]   _____
Tenant Improvements [area x $_____ per s.f.]   _____
Builder's Overhead/Profit   _____
Contingency (3-5%, excl. land)   _____ [1]

Total Hard Costs $_____

Soft Costs
Architectural & Engineering $_____
Survey & Soils   _____
Permits & Fees   _____
Insurance [CofC] and Property Taxes   _____
Legal & Accounting   _____
Title & Recording   _____
Leasing Commissions   _____ [2]
Construction Loan Fee   _____ [3]
Appraisal & Inspection Fee   _____
Loan Broker Fee [points], if applicable   _____
Developer's Overhead   _____
Marketing & Promotion   _____
Construction & Lease-up Loan Interest   _____ [4]
Contingency   _____ [5]

Total Soft Costs $_____

TOTAL PROJECT COSTS   **$1,000,000**

LOAN AMOUNT TO BE 80% (OR 85%?) OF PROJECT COST   **$ 800,000**

[1]   Included as "soft cost" if developer is owner/builder, or may be
      deferred until completion and/or lease-up
[2]   5 year lease [normally] = 25% of 1st year's income;
      10 yr. lease = 37-1/2%
[3]   1-2% for 12-36 month term
[4]   Typically 60-65% of the average outstanding loan balance
[5]   Lender may put 3-5% here, typically. Soft cost varies on product
      type or perceived cost. This can offset developer's overhead,
      supervision, etc.

**WHAT IS THE ESTIMATING PHILOSOPHY OF THE DEVELOPER AND LENDER?
CONSERVATIVE OR OPTIMISTIC?**

FINANCE PRINCIPLES [continued]

WORKSHEET - ANALYZING THE PROJECT [continued]:

ECONOMIC FEASIBILITY/LOAN AMOUNT
FEASIBILITY

Gross Income - Rents	$_____
Other Income [Parking, Laundry, Vending, etc.]	_____
Total Gross Income	_____
Vacancy - usually @ 5%	_____

EFFECTIVE GROSS INCOME $_____

LESS EXPENSES   [_____]

NET OPERATING INCOME [NOI] $ 110,000

MARKET CAP RATE   9.5%

VALUE $ 1,158,000

LOAN AMOUNT [70-75%] **Use 75%** $ 868,000

Loan Coverage [cross check]

Net Operating Income [per above]	$ 110,000
Debt Service Coverage Ratio	1.15%
Income Available to Service Debt [annual]	95,650
Loan Constant 10.75%, 30 yr.	11.21%

LOAN AMOUNT $ 854,000

NOTE: Cost controls the Loan Amount in this example
* Vacancy factor applied even if single tenant building

NOTE: THE LOAN AMOUNT WILL BE THE LESSER OF THE AMOUNT DETERMINED BY [a] COST, [b] ECONOMIC FEASIBILITY, OR [c] LOAN COVERAGE. In "reasonable" economic times, the loan amount will be determined by the cost or economic feasibility, not loan coverage

OTHER FACTORS VIEWED BY LENDER, NOT QUANTIFIED:
Location Analysis
Site Analysis
Improvement Analysis

DISCUSS M&M OFFICE BUILDING

Borrower	$1,000,000 vanished on paper.
Tenant[s]	How [and where] did it go?
Contractor	Interest rates increased greatly.
Source of Repayment	Lease rates dropped from $1.25 to $1.00

OTHER FACTORS FOR DEVELOPER
Required Equity
Return on Equity
"Residual Value" - Net Income/Cap Rate less Total Cost

FINANCE PRINCIPLES [continued]

INDEX OF SUPPORTING DOCUMENTS
GENERALLY STANDARD WITH LENDERS

Initial Loan Package - Preliminary   Make initial package as complete as possible.

I.   Initial Preparation/Presentation

    1.   Financial Statements:
        a.   Borrower - 3 years' prior statements and Federal Tax Returns.
        b.   Principals - 3 years' prior statements and Federal Tax Returns.
    2.   Plans and Specifications final for construction.
    3.   Legal Description of subject property and any additional collateral.
    4.   Preliminary Title Report, CC&R's and Title Exceptions.
    5.   Purchase Price and date purchased of subject property and any additional collateral.
    6.   Project Pro Forma (Project Budget and Economic Analysis forms) signed by owner including:
        a.   Total Project Cost Recap including costs paid to date.
        b.   Proposed Rental Schedule.
        c.   Estimated Operating Expenses
    7.   Signed Building Leases (if applicable) and standard lease form.
    8.   Ground Lease (if applicable).
    9.   Takeout commitment from permanent lender (if applicable).
    10.   Land Purchase Escrow Instructions.
    11.   Phase I Environmental Report; lender may order directly

II.   Required Prior to Closing [Complete Loan Package]

    1.   Financial Statements
        a.   Contractor - 1 or more year's prior statements and Federal Tax Return.
        b.   Lessee - 1 or more years' prior statements.
    2.   Formation Documents: Partnership Agreement, Recorded Statement of Partnership, Copy of Borrowers' Fictitious Business name Statement and all amendments thereto; LLC/LLP Operating Agreements.
    3.   Articles of Incorporation, By-Laws and Corporate Resolution to Borrow.
    4.   Construction Contracts including referral list of major sub-contractors and contractors.
    5.   Copies of bids and all executed subcontracts.
    6.   Survey.
    7.   Soils Report.
    8.   Building permit.
    9.   If lien priority will be broken by starting construction before Bank's Trust Deed would record, make sure title company is on board for an Indemnity Agreement.
    10.   Proposed parcel map.
    11.   If any Trust Deeds on subject property are to be paid off concurrently with the recording of the Bank's Trust Deed, supply information to title company to ask for a demand or notify Bank of location of escrow.
    12.   Fire Insurance as required by lender.
    13.   Copy of Public Liability and Property Damage insurance as required by lender.
    14.   Copy of Workers' Compensation Insurance.
    15.   Engineering Report addressing structural soundness of subject project (if applicable).
    16.   Performance and Payment Bonds for General Contractor or Sub-Contractors (if applicable).

NAPA VALLEY GATEWAY BUSINESS PARK

A Development of **PACIFIC UNION**

A 386 Acre Mixed-Use Master Planned Development

MASTER PLAN

Sales & Leasing Office
499 Devlin Rd.
Napa, CA 94558
(707) 252-8533
Fax (707) 252-8793

A Development of **PACIFIC UNION**

NAPA VALLEY GATEWAY BUSINESS PARK
Since 1988

NORTH KELLY ROAD

SOUTH KELLY ROAD

STATE HWY. 12 (JAMESON CANYON)

STATE HWY. 29 & 12

STATE HWY. 29 & 12

DEVLIN RD.

GATEWAY RD. EAST

GATEWAY RD. WEST

GATEWAY ROAD

AIRPORT BLVD.

AIRPORT BLVD.

ALEXIS COURT

TECHNOLOGY WAY

TECHNOLOGY COURT

HARLOW COURT

AIRPARK RD.

N

Lot labels:
- 1 — 4.3 AC
- 2 — 2.1 AC
- 3 — 2.2 AC
- 46 — 3.5 AC
- 45 — 2.5 AC
- 43 — 2.7 AC
- 44 — 3.1 AC
- 42 — 2.8 AC
- 39 — 2.9 AC
- 40 — 2.1 AC
- 41 — 2.5 AC
- 38 — 2.5 AC
- 37 — 2.5 AC
- 36 — 2.6 AC
- 11 — 3.3 AC
- 35 — 3.1 AC
- 55 — 4.4 AC
- 34 — 3.0 AC
- 17 — 3.2 AC
- 20 — 3.2 AC
- 54 — 2.7 AC
- 53 — 2.7 AC
- 52 — 2.9 AC
- 31 — 2.5 AC
- 29 — 3.3 AC
- 21 — 2.5 AC
- 22 — 2.7 AC
- 23 — 2.6 AC
- 70 — 2.9 AC
- 72 — 2.6 AC
- 73 — 1.9 AC
- 74 — 3.6 AC
- 26 — 3.4 AC
- 78 — 3.7 AC
- 25 — 2.4 AC

Callout boxes:

Future Vineyards 22 acres

A.P. Tech 75,000 sf + 10 acres Precision valves and regulators

IBEW/NECA Electricians' apprenticeship training facility 16,000 sf

NVG R&D/Office 16,000 sf

OddzOn/CAP Toys (Hasbro) 400,000 sf 19 acres Office, R&D, Warehouse

Wine Services Co-op 104,000 sf

NAPA COUNTY AIRPORT

G&W Management 87,000 sf total Industrial/Warehouse

G&W Management Industrial/Warehouse 76,000 sf total

Santen Inc. 40,000 sf (1st Phase) + 13 acres Ophthalmic pharmaceuticals

G&W Management Office/Flex 72,500 sf total

"Ranch House" Sales & Leasing Office Napa Valley Gateway 60,000 sf total R&D/Office

Service Center Business Suite's Inn & Commercial/Service

The Doctors Company 78,000 sf Insurance

Napa County Fire Station

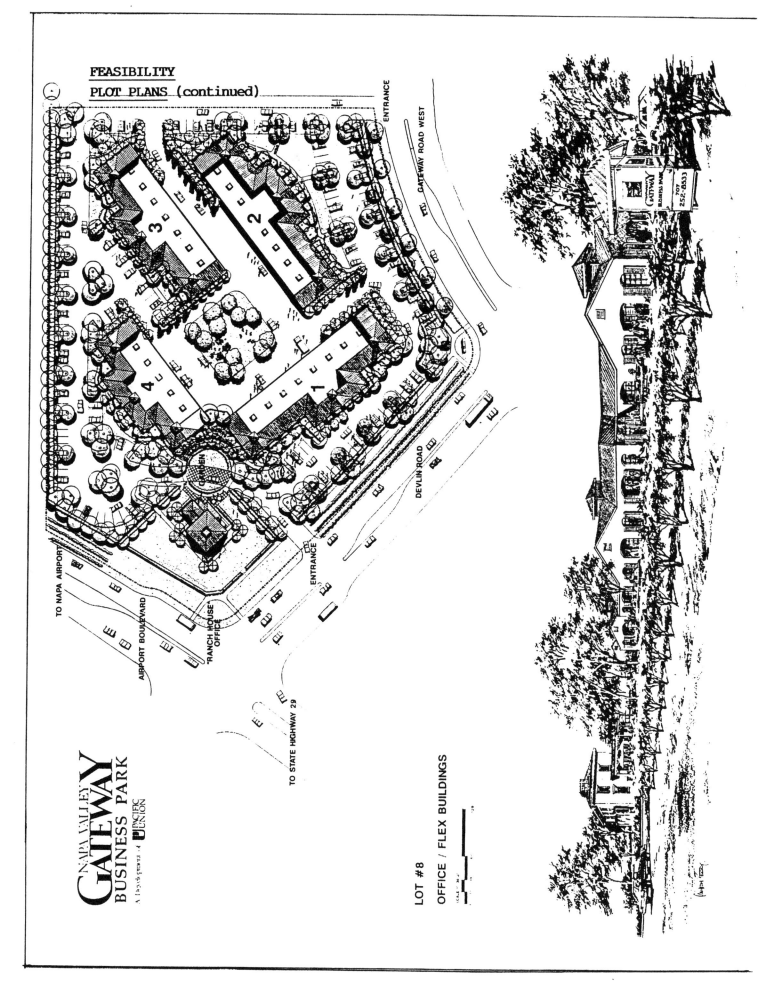

NAPA VALLEY
GATEWAY
BUSINESS PARK
A Development of PACIFIC UNION

LOT #8

OFFICE / FLEX BUILDINGS

ENTRANCE

GATEWAY ROAD WEST

DEVLIN ROAD

ENTRANCE

TO NAPA AIRPORT

AIRPORT BOULEVARD

"RANCH HOUSE" OFFICE

TO STATE HIGHWAY 29

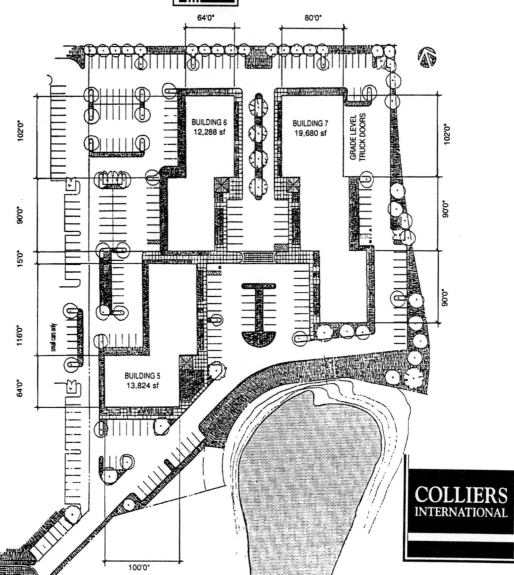

Building 5: 13,824 Square Feet
Building 6: 12,288 Square Feet
Building 7: 19,680 Square Feet

For more information contact:
Brooks Pedder or Phil Garrett
424 Executive Court North, Suite D
Fairfield, California 94585
Tel: 707/863-0188
Fax: 707/863-0181

♦	Location:	Executive Court North (north side of lake)
♦	Site:	Approximately 4.79 acres (22% coverage)
♦	Parking:	**4.67 parking spaces per 1,000 rentable square feet**
♦	Column Spacing:	30' width on average
♦	Power:	1200 amps @ 120/208 volts to each building
♦	Clearance:	12' minimum ceiling height
♦	Loading:	Three (3) 10' wide x 12' high grade level doors at northeast end of Building 7. Additional grade level door(s) can be added at north end of Building 6.
♦	Divisibility:	Divisible to suit

F A I R F I E L D   C O R P O R A T E   C O M M O N S

LONE TREE OFFICE PARK

LUCKING AND VLAHOS DEVELOPER

3200 LONE TREE WAY ANTIOCH, CA.

ELEVATION FROM LONE TREE WAY

32,000 s.f. of offices on 2.5 acres

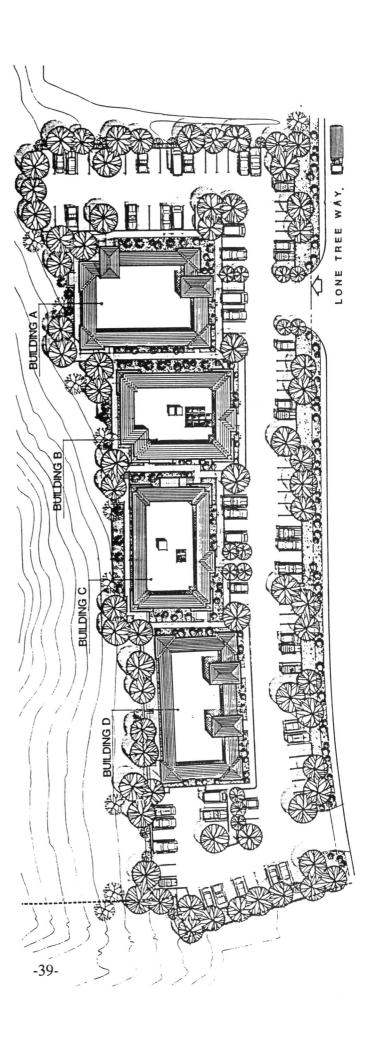

BUILDING A

BUILDING B

BUILDING C

BUILDING D

LONE TREE WAY.

FEASIBILITY

CASE STUDY

THE BACKGROUND

Ronald Retail [Seller] decides to retire and sell his building from which he has operated his business for several years. The building is owned free and clear and is located in a prime suburban location. The total floor area is 18,500 s.f.; approximately 40% of which is not located on the ground floor. David Developer [Buyer] is an old friend of Ronald's and they negotiate for the purchase of the building. There is no brokerage referral/commission on the purchase. Buyer is an experienced developer, well acquainted with renovations of this type. He needs to be as there are substantial code and cosmetic upgrades to be done to the building.

THE PURCHASE CONTRACT

Buyer negotiates a purchase price of $1,400,000 "as-is". The contract provides that the price will be "reviewed" should renovation cost exceed $250,000. Buyer has one year to obtain the necessary entitlements prior to closing escrow on the building. Seller receives no earnest money until the close of escrow.

A few weeks following execution of the purchase agreement, Buyer's architect estimates renovation costs to be $483,000. Market retail/rental rates [NNN] in the area are $1.25 per s.f. [minimum] with upper office space comparables at $1.00 per s.f. or slightly less. A fee appraisal [MAI] of $1,550,000 [9 1/2% cap rate] was done two years previously.

THE LEASE/PURCHASE OPTION

Through services of a broker, Buyer negotiates a lease with a Good Tenant who wishes to expand into the area. The Tenant has several outlets in the Bay Area and is [relatively] strong financially. Buyer also negotiates a purchase option with Tenant. The lease and purchase option terms are noted below:

Note: Amounts are annual rents. Three [3] months free rent during the
1st year. Ten [10] year lease term. Rents are NNN.

*1st	-	$135,000 [$.81]		6th	-	$219,780 [$.99]
*2nd	-	187,200 [$.84]		7th	-	228,974 [1.03]
*3rd	-	194,760 [$.88]	LEASE	8th	-	238,620 [1.07]
4th	-	203,778 [$.91]		9th	-	248,748 [1.12]
5th	-	211,033 [$.95]		10th	-	259,380 [1.17]

*33 mos = $172,300 per yr.

During 3rd year -   OPTION   During 4th year -
  $2,300,000 $2,415,000
  [$124/s.f.]   [$130/s.f.]

Good Tenant does all of the renovation work at its sole cost with only minimal expense to Buyer.

METHODS OF VALUATION

a. Replacement cost
   NOTE: due to the complexity of the structure, detailed quantity takeoffs were not made, and this [type of analysis] will not be used herein
b. Capitalization rate   Ranging between 8 1/2%-9 1/2%
c. Discounted cash flow   Formula is: 1 divided by $[1 + i]^n$: where i = rate; n = number of years; to the nth power

FEASIBILITY

CASE STUDY (continued)

THE QUESTIONS
1. Compute the economic value based upon:
    a. Discounted cash flow at 8% and 10%
    b. The appropriate capitalization rates
2. How much value do you place on the appraiser's report?
3. Would this be a "keeper" or developed for resale?
4. **Would you have made this deal?**

OTHER COMMENTS

Discounted Cash Flow
* 8% = $1,379,000
  10% = $1,253,000
  without residual value at end of 10th year

Capitalization Rates
    8 1/2% = $2,027,000
    9 %   = $1,915,000
    9 1/2% = $1,814,000

* Approximately $2,200,000 if option exercised; both for 8% and 10%
  The rental reduction is much greater than the "mark-up" value of the inferior improvements.
  Good tenant negotiated a terrific deal!

FEASIBILITY

TRUE/FALSE EXAM

T F 1. The average commercial real estate loan in California is approximately $10,000,000

T F 2. The "process" of RE Development is more circular than linear, as in manufacturing

T F 3. One of the most dramatic changes in RE Development in more than a decade is the [virtual] elimination of 100% financing

T F 4. The other dramatic change is the tremendous pressure of supply to place institutional funds into real estate investments, although not with the intensity of the '80's

T F 5. RE Development still requires intuition, common sense, and "gut feelings" in addition to scientific analyses

T F 6. It is relatively easy to obtain financing with off-shore sources if one is experienced in development

T F 7. A project has a cost of $1,000,000, $100,000 annual net income, and commands a market cap rate of 9.25%. The economic value, then, is $925,000

T F 8. Gross amounts [raw numbers] are the most important items in beginning a market analysis or survey

T F 9. The five Basic Elements of RE Development are: Land, Use/User, Permits, Marketability, and Financing

T F 10. It is difficult to be both a contractor <u>and</u> a developer

T F 11. RE Development basically is a macro market and an economy of the few

T F 12. Intrinsic value or replacement cost <u>always</u> may be out of synchchronization with the economic value of real estate

T F 13. If a job starts "sour" it will probably continue that way unless work is stopped to resolve the problem[s]

T F 14. It is not of paramount importance that a seller of property understand the timing or details in processing a use permit

T F 15. In Sacramento, typically, the buyer pays for title insurance

T F 16. The development risks of "Market", "Construction/Permits", and "Financing" are dynamic, not static

T F 17. Depending upon one's experience, some of the procedural steps in RE Development may be eliminated

T F 18. Market knowledge is more important than market analysis

T F 19. Exclusive of the Zoning Administrator, a Planning Staff has no vote in the permit process <u>after</u> an application has been accepted as complete

T F 20. General plan zoning and actual or specific plan zoning are the same

T F 21. You may proceed with your design and use permit submittals while the EIR is being processed, understanding there is a substantial $$$ risk

T F 22. The best source for loans under $1,000,000 is a statewide bank with many offices

FEASIBILITY

TRUE/FALSE EXAM (continued)

T F 23. A mortgagor is the borrower

T F 24. Construction lenders always look at the real estate value first

T F 25. For a $1,000,000 construction loan at 12% interest, the interest for one year with a 60% use factor will be $72,000

T F 26. The amount of the construction loan will be based solely upon the cost of construction

T F 27. In a lender's analysis, vacancy factors are not applied to single tenant properties in computing the loan amount

T F 28. Currently, lenders require an excess of 10-25% of computed net income over the loan amortization payments

T F 29. Economic analysis always is done ahead of market analysis

T F 30. Responses to written marketing questionnaires, may tend to be lowest in May, June, July, and December

T F 31. Expert market analysis sometimes makes recommendations which go beyond the available raw data

T F 32. Forecasts are often projections of what has happened already

T F 33. Marketing research is the systematic gathering , recording, and analyzing of data about problems relating to the marketing of products

T F 34. In marketing research, a symptom would be the rental rate is too high; a problem would be that the property is not leasing

T F 35. Market analysis analyzes the components of demand

T F 36. Marketability studies determine absorption without consideration of economic viability

T F 37. Feasibility studies include the total picture, including economic viability

T F 38. Large or small projects can fail for the same reason - a lack of proper market analysis

T F 39. The broker who first tells a developer about a "deal" is entitled to the commission under procuring cause

T F 40. By shrewd negotiating, one never need pay more than a 4% brokerage commission on land or investment properties

Development Review Checklist

Prepared by Gary Binger
Planning Director
Association of Bay Area Governments (A.B.A.G.)

The following criteria can be used to quickly evaluate the site planning and design quality of small and mid-sized development proposals. This approach is intended to provide an even level of review and to avoid overlooking certain key factors.

Buildings and Site Planning

		Yes	No	Unsure	NA
1.	Architectural quality is as good or better than surroundings.	0	0	0	0
2.	Building materials and colors are compatible with surroundings.	0	0	0	0
3.	Development signing is shown and blends well into building and site design.	0	0	0	0
4.	On-site lighting does not impact neighboring property.	0	0	0	0
5.	Parking areas are well-screened by earthmounding, landscaping or low walls.	0	0	0	0
6.	Loading and trash collection areas are located to side or rear of development or are well-screened.	0	0	0	0

Circulation

1.	Minimum number of driveways onto adjacent streets.	0	0	0	0
2.	Street access points line up with median openings and/or access points on opposite side of the street.	0	0	0	0
3.	Corner developments emphasize auto access on local or side streets rather than primary arterials.	0	0	0	0
4.	Acceleration/deceleration lanes are provided for major traffic generators on busy arterials.	0	0	0	0
5.	Loading/servicing areas located to minimize traffic flow disruption.	0	0	0	0
6.	Pedestrian on and off-site network effectively connects all major activities.	0	0	0	0

Landscaping and Grading

1.	Landscaping emphasized in areas with highest visibility.	0	0	0	0
2.	Development minimizes removal of large existing trees.	0	0	0	0

SAMPLE - INDUSTRIAL OR OFFICE BUILDING

MEMORANDUM OF INTENT

This memorandum, when executed by Lessee and Lessor, shall constitute a binding agreement subject only to (a) Lessee's execution of a definitive Lease, a copy of which has been furnished Lessee, and (b) Lessor's obtaining the required use and building permits from the appropriate jurisdiction(s).

PREMISES
The subject Premises consists of _____
_____
and is more particularly described on Exhibit "A", attached hereto.

TERM OF LEASE
The Term and rental obligation will commence upon issuance of the Certificate of Occupancy by the
_____. The Term of the Lease shall be for a period of _____ years.

RENT ADJUSTMENT
Commencing with the _____ month of the Term, the Rent shall be adjusted pursuant to the Consumer Price Index (CPI) as delineated in paragraph _____ of the Lease. The annual change so calculated shall be limited to a cumulative 7% increase (but no decrease).

IMPROVEMENTS
Lessor shall, at its sole cost and expense, complete construction of the improvements per Lessee's requirements as more particularly described on Exhibit "B" - Outline Specifications and Finish Schedule attached hereto.

LEASING COMMISSION
Lessor shall pay any applicable real estate commissions at rates which are usual and customary for this type of usage in _____ County.

SECURITY DEPOSIT
Upon execution of the Lease, Lessee shall pay Lessor the first month's Base Rental, as defined below, which amount shall be applied to the last month's rental of the Term hereof.

BASE RENT
Pursuant to the foregoing and Paragraph _____ of the Lease, the Base Rent shall be _____ per month.

This memorandum is effective upon the date of Lessor's acceptance and shall continue in effect until the earlier of (a) execution of a definitive Lease by Lessee and Lessor, or (b) thirty (30) days from Lessor's acceptance hereof.

Accepted by:

LESSEE_____   LESSOR_____

    By_____   By_____
       Its   Its

DATE_____   DATE_____

Add, if appropriate:

LEASE OFFER   The offer of this Lease is subject to Lessor's leasing additional space within the development at terms and conditions satisfactory to Lessor at its sole discretion, and is further subject to Lessor obtaining the necessary permits required by _____ or other authorities having jurisdiction, for construction of the project.

OUTLINE SPECIFICATIONS

Pursuant to the Memorandum of Intent, Lessee shall approve the working drawings as they are being prepared. Lessor shall provide the site plan and "building footprint" to Lessee at the earliest possible time. The working drawings, when completed, shall be incorporated into the Lease.

GENERAL

Construction of the Premises having a total area of _____ with an improved office area of _____. The Premises are part of a building having an overall area of _____.
The scope of work does include development of off-site improvements - i.e., utility extension(s) to property lines, curb, gutter, and sidewalks, and related items, unless specifically noted on the plans. Zoning to permit the construction of a Type V-N building with an F-2 occupancy (service, storage, assembly, and offices).

STRUCTURAL

Varco-Pruden Building System, with a minimum clear height of 18'-0" beneath the beams. The structural beams and columns are designed for roof loads only, excluding any conveyors, cranes, or similar equipment. The WWM reinforced concrete floor shall be 5" thick, with a smooth troweled finish.
Architectural details....paneling, hardwall, fenestrations, and colors... as provided by _____
_____. The office area will be wood/metal stud framed walls; the framed ceiling is not designed as a "rated structural ceiling".

ELECTRICAL

_____ amp, 208 volt, 3Ø service and main panel. Office outlets placed as required by Code. Office lighting to be provided at 80 fc; other areas at 25 fc (eye level). Exterior security lighting is included. This section includes connections to mechanical and plumbing equipment furnished under other sections of the work, including irrigation timers. Internal security systems (ADT, etc.), distribution of service other than within the office, Muzak or intercom connections, telephone, illuminated signs, or other special requirements not otherwise listed herein are excluded.

FIRE SPRINKLERS

Ordinary hazard, Group III. Detection checks, PIV, and interior fire hose racks as may be required by the Fire Marshall having jurisdiction. Meter connection fees are included. Fire hydrant(s), wall mounted fire extinguishers, and a "central service monitoring station" are excluded.

HEATING, VENTILATION, AND AIR-CONDITIONING

Single zone, heated and air-conditioned office area, designed with good area practice and custom; bathroom exhaust and roof vents per Code; gas fired space heater in warehouse area. Extend condensate drains to roof gutter/DS.

PLUMBING

Connections and installation of gas, sewer, and water service of adequate capacity to serve the Premises in the intended use. Install 40 gal. electric water heater with pan. Bathroom - 1 ea. Lav (wall mounted), installed to HDCP Code. Distribution and/or extension of additional services within the Premises is excluded.

SITE GRADING AND PAVING

Provide base rock and/or recompaction beneath the building slab of sufficient thickness, consistent with good design and per the soils engineer's report and recommendation. Site grading is estimated to "balance" - i.e., no importing of fill dirt. On site storm drainage is included. All paving sections designed for automobile and light truck traffic.

LANDSCAPING

Designed by a licensed landscape architect with an eye to low maintenance costs, commensurate with quality treatment. All landscaped areas to have an automatically controlled irrigation system.

Page 1 of 3

MISCELLANEOUS

DRIVEWAYS	Curb cut driveway(s) as noted on the plans
ROOFING	20 year rating
TRUCK DOORS	12' x 14' - "coil away"
WINDOWS/ENTRY	Bronze anodized aluminum; solar grey glass
INSULATION	R-1 and R-19 as required by Title 24 Code
TRASH ENCLOSURE	As required by Code
SECURITY FENCING	
SKYLIGHTS	
FLOOR COVERINGS	
WALL COVERINGS	
DRAPERIES	
FURNITURE	

Donald Trump, "The Art of the Deal":
One of the first things which anyone should learn
about real estate and New York real estate in particular -
is never to sign a letter of intent. Years can be spent
in court trying to get out of a seemingly simple and
"non-binding" agreement.

Page 2 of 3

-47-

INITIAL

FINISH SCHEDULE EXHIBIT "B"

OUTLINE SPECIFICATIONS FOR_____

ROOM	FLOOR					WALLS								CEILING					
	CONCRETE, UNSEALED	CONCRETE, SEALED	VINYL COMP. TILE	CARPET		SHEETROCK, UNPAINTED	SHEETROCK, PAINTED	CONCRETE, UNPAINTED	CONCRETE, PAINTED	WALL PANELING	WALL COVERING	MARLITE WAINSCOTE		SUSPENDED T-BAR	FOIL INSULATION	SHEETROCK, UNPAINTED	SHEETROCK, PAINTED		

NOTE: 1. *All suspended ceiling heights to be _____*
        2. *Visqueen moisture barrier beneath office slab only.*
        3. *All office doors to be 7'-0" high*

Page 3 of 3

INITIAL

THE EXPERIENCE CURVE

At the conclusion of World War II and into the late 1940's, government industrial engineers [then called "efficiency experts"] and economists discovered a significant increase in effectiveness or cost reduction the more repetitions there were in a particular process. They also discovered that there were finite boundaries to the process, and that the results were rather clearly predictable. The analysis originally was applied only to manufacturing processes. However, in the 1960's it began to be applied more broadly, as the Japanese picked up on the phenomenon.

This process or phenomenon is called the **"Experience Curve"**. And simply stated the theorem is: **There is a 20-30% increase in productivity/decrease in cost during each time the number of repetitions is doubled**. The base **originates from zero experience.** And in today's world, it is difficult to start from a true base of zero experience. For example, in applying this to real estate development, land is extended very far on the experience curve; it has been around forever! Similarly, your plumber may be working on his 2,000th repetition. Therefore, there will have to be another 2,000 "repetitions" before any significant savings or increased efficiency is achieved. However, there are several elements in real estate development, which through the inclusion of experienced "consultants", to which the experience curve is applicable. Such items can include: [a] permit processing, [b] planning and design, [c] construction, [d] financing, and [e] many of the contractual requirements, or the legal aspects.

I am advised of the classical case of Black & Decker [a proponent] and Skil. I have had my own recent experience in advertising costs for workshops which I produce. Certainly, you have had your own personal encounter with an "experience curve". In the case of Black and Decker, the emphasis was on quality increase for the same dollars, rather than strictly a reduction in price.

While there is no promise that the experience curve will happen precisely, it is very, very likely that if you don't pay heed to it, someone else will!

Why does the experience curve happen?

      1. <u>Learning</u>   * 3. <u>Method - better way?</u>
      2. <u>Economies of scale</u>   * 4. <u>Tooling; equipment; machinery</u>
            * <u>most likely when curve begins to flatten out</u> ❶

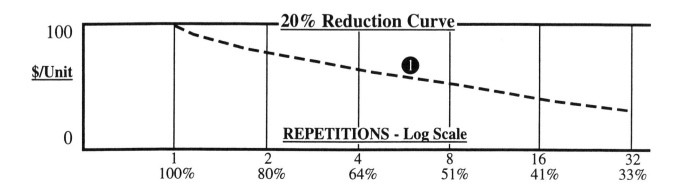

SOURCE MATERIALS AND READING LIST

FORMS, CONTRACTS, TECHNICAL BOOKS

Builders Booksource
1817 Fourth Street
Berkeley, CA 94710
[510] 845-6874

Builders Booksource
Ghirardelli Square
San Francisco, CA 94109
[415] 440-5773

The Urban Land Institute
1025 Thos. Jefferson St. NW #500W
Washington, DC 20007-5201
[800] 321-5011

Stacey's Technical Books
581 Market Street
San Francisco, CA 94105
[415] 421-4687

PERIODICALS

Far too many to list herein ... and some come and go in the publishing business. Check the library, above noted sources, large law firms, large contracting firms, property management firms, etc. for a particular topic...or call me if you really get stuck.

COSTS AND ESTIMATING

Saylor Consulting Group
12 Geary St. - 7th Floor
San Francisco, CA 94108
[415] 291-3200

R.S. Means Company, Inc.
100 Construction Plaza
PO Box 800
Kingston, MA 02364
[781] 585-7880
[800] 448-8182

REFERENCE BOOKS

"Property Development" 3rd Ed., John McMahan, McGraw-Hill
"The Art of the Deal" Donald J. Trump, Random House
"The Art of the Comeback" Donald J. Trump, Random House
"Real Estate Development; Principles and Process", Mike E. Miles, The Urban Land Institute
"Professional Real Estate Development; The U.L.I. Guide to the Business", Richard B. Peiser,
    Dearborn Financial Publishers
"The Complete Real Estate Advisor", Daniel J. deBenedictis, Pocket Books
"The California Real Estate Primer" 42nd Ed., Ray D. Westcott, Real Estate Primer
    Publishers
Varied and Miscellaneous Publications, The Urban Land Institute (U.L.I.), address and
    phone noted above

NOTE: The real estate sections of Barnes & Noble, B. Dalton, Waldenbooks and Borders, etc., carry books mostly about remodeling or buying/selling a house. However they can order many of these listed books.
Builders Booksource usually stocks many of the books noted herein; otherwise they are readily available from their distributors on short notice.

SOURCE MATERIALS AND READING LIST (continued)

PROFESSIONAL AND TRADE ASSOCIATIONS

Building Industry Association [BIA] of No. California
200 Porter Dr. #200; P.O. Box 5160
San Ramon, CA 94583
[925] 820-7626
        affiliate Nat'l. Assn. of Home Builders (NAHB)

National Assoc. of Industrial and Office Parks (NAIOP)
SiliconValley Chapter
2911 Queens Estates
San Jose, CA 95135
[408] 452-1634

The Urban Land Institute (ULI)
1025 Thos. Jefferson St. NW, Suite 500W
Washington, DC 20007-5201
[800] 321-5011; [202] 624-7000

Builder Owners and Managers Association (BOMA)
465 California St., Suite 504
San Francisco, CA 94104
[415] 362-8567

Institute of Real Estate Management (IREM)
Hearst Building (3rd and Market) Suite 1132
San Francisco, CA 94103
[415] 243-9313
        costs and expenses for all types of projects

American Society of Real Estate Counselors
430 No. Michigan Avenue
Chicago, IL 60611-4089
[312] 329-8427

California Business Properties Association
1932 "J" Street, Suite 260
Sacramento, CA 95814
[916] 443-4676

Commercial Lease Law Insider
Brownstone Publishers, Inc.
149 Fifth Avenue
New York, NY 10010
[212] 473-8200

SOURCE MATERIALS AND READING LIST (continued)

PERMIT PROCESSING

Complete Planning Commissioner's Handbook
League of California Cities
1400 "K" Street
Sacramento, CA 95814

Subdivision Map Act Manual
Daniel J. Curtin, Jr.   Daniel J. Curtin, Jr.
Solano Press   McCutchen, Doyle, Brown & Enersen
P.O. Box 773   P.O. Box V
Point Arena, CA 95468   Walnut Creek, CA 94596-1270
[707] 884-4508   [925] 937-8000

California Land-Use and Planning Law
Daniel J. Curtin, Jr.
Solano Press (per above)

The California Environmental Quality Act, June 1986 (CEQA) and updates
Governor's Office of Planning and Research
Office of Permit Assistance - OPR Publications
[916] 322-4245

Guide to the California Environmental Quality Act (CEQA)
Michael H. Remy, Tina A. Thomas, Sharon E. Duggan, James G. Moose
Solano Press (per above)

NOTE: Most publications are revised annually or biannually

CONSULTING AND PROFESSIONAL ASSOCIATIONS

American Arbitration Association (AAA)   Associated General Contractors (AGC)
255 Bush Street - 18th Floor   1390 Willow Pass Road, Suite 1030
San Francisco, CA 94104   Concord, CA 94520
(415) 981-3901   (925) 827-2422

American Institute of Achitects (AIA)   Consulting Engineers and Land
130 Sutter Street, Suite 600   Surveyors of California (CELSOC)
San Francisco, CA 94104   1303 "J" Street, Suite 370
(415) 362-7397   Sacramento, CA 95814
                                                (916) 441-7991

ESTOPPEL STATEMENT [sample]

ATTENTION: RE: Lease Dated:

                                     Landlord:

                                     Tenant:

                                     Premises:

Gentlemen:

The undersigned, Tenant in the above referenced lease, hereby confirms, as of the date hereof, the following:

1.   That it is in full and complete possession of the demised premises, such possession having been delivered by the Landlord and having been accepted by the undersigned.

2.   That the improvements and space required to be furnished by the terms of the Lease have been completed in all respects to the satisfaction of the undersigned and are open for the use of the undersigned, its customers, employees, and invitees.

3.   That all duties of an inducement nature required of the Landlord in said Lease have been fulfilled.

4.   That said Lease is in full force and effect; that there is no existing default on the part of the Landlord in the terms thereof; and that said Lease has not been amended, modified, supplemented or superseded except as follows:

5.   That no rents have been prepaid except as provided by said Lease; that the undersigned does not now have or hold any claim against Landlord which might be set off or credited against future accruing rents.

6.   That the undersigned has received no notice of a prior sale, transfer, assignment, hypothecation or pledge of the said Lease or of the rents secured therein, except to you.

7.   That rents provided in the Lease commenced to accrue on _____

                              TENANT:

                              By: _____

                                   Its

                              Date: _____

SOURCE:
1995 CEQA Guidelines
Appendix A

CEQA PROCESS FLOW CHART

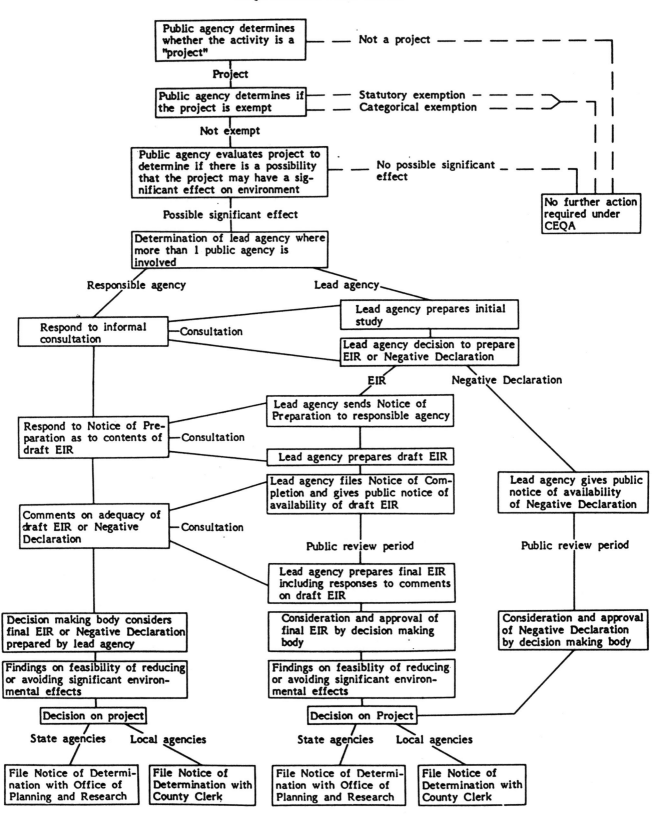

NOTE: This flow chart is intended merely to illustrate the EIR process contemplated by these Guidelines. The language contained in the Guidelines controls in case of discrepancies.

Supplementary Document C

TIME PERIODS FOR REVIEW
OF ENVIRONMENTAL DOCUMENTS

Document or Action	*Effect*	*Time Period*	*CEQA Guidelines*
Review of application for completeness.	If no determination is made within this period, it will be deemed complete.	30 days	15101
Lead Agency acceptance of a project as complete.	Begins maximum one year period to complete environmental review for certain projects.	1 year	15060
Initial Study.	Provides 30 days to determine whether an EIR or Neg Dec will be required.	30 days	15102
Notice of Preparation.	Provides 30 days from receipt of NOP for agencies to review and comment.	30 days	15103
Convening of Scope and Content meetings.	Requires a meeting requested by an agency or by the applicant to be convened within 30 days of the request.	30 days	15104
Public Review.	When an environmental document is submitted to the Clearinghouse, the public review period shall be at least as long as the review set by the Clearinghouse.	EIR: 30-90 days ND: 21 days to a "reasonable time."	15105
Review by State Agencies.	Provides standard 45 days for EIR's and standard 30 days for NDs.	EIR: 45 days ND: 30 days	15106
Completion of negative declaration.	For a private project, the Neg Dec must be completed in 105 days.	105 days	15107
Completion and certification of EIR.	For a private project, an EIR must be completed within one year. May be extended once for up to 90 days.	1 year	15108
Notice of Determination — filing.	Provides that the notice shall be filed within 5 days (local agencies only).	5 days	15094
Notice of Determination.	Filing starts a 180-day statute of limitations to court challenges to the approval of the project.	180 days	15094

Document or Action	Effect	Time Period	CEQA Guidelines
Suspension of time limits.	Unreasonable delay of document preparation caused by the applicant allows suspension of time period in Guidelines, Sections 15107 & 15108.	varies	15109
Projects with federal involvement.	Time limits may be waived or superseded by federal time requirements.		15110

NOTE: *Related time periods for project approval are contained in Chapter 4.5 of the Government Code beginning at Section 65920. These generally run concurrently with certain CEQA time periods.*

Source: Kosta & Zischke, Practice Under the California Environmental Quality Act (CEB 1997 Update, p. 1267, Sup Doc. C)

"Pollution is nothing but resources we're not harvesting." **Buckminster Fuller**

G L O S S A R Y

AAA   American Arbitration Association

ABAG   Association of Bay Area Governments. Responsible [ostensibly] for overall planning with the 7 Bay Area Counties, (now expanded to 9), although its Planning Director was quoted as saying, "The job is like herding cats!"

Absorption   The amount of space or units consumed [sold or leased] within a finite period of time, usually one year.

ADR   Alternative Dispute Resolution

A&E   Architectural and Engineering

AGC   Associated General Contrators

AIA   American Institute of Architects

APR   Annual Percentage Rate

ARM Loans   Adjustable rate mortgage loans

BCDC   Bay Conservation and Development Commission; tidelands approvals; jurisdiction 100' from tidelands [as defined] and the entire waters of San Francisco Bay.

Bridge Loan   Short term [3-5 year] interim loan on completed facility; generally interest only. Also called "mini-perm". See "bullet loan".

Build-to-Suit   Project developed to client's or tenant's specific needs or requirements. Also called "turnkey", as "give them the key and they move in".

Bullet Loan   Short term [3-5 year] interim loan on completed facility to let the income stream become stabilized or seasoned - e.g., offices and shopping centers. The terms "bridge", "gap", "bullet", and "mini-perm" are used interchangeably.

Capitalization [Cap] Rate   The rate of return by which the marketplace values a particular type of real estate project. The cap rate is divided into the net annual income; not multiplied by the cost.

CC&R's   Conditions, Covenants, and Restrictions

CELSOC   Consulting Engineers and Land Surveyors of California

CEQA   California Environmental Quality Act; legislation enacted in early 1970's from which the current environmental processing is derived.

CM   Construction Management or Manager

CofC Insurance   Course of Construction insurance; owner's policy for fire, liability, and extended coverage endorsements. Obtained by the party having insurable interest.

CofO   Certificate of occupancy

Construction Financing   Short term [usually up to 3 years] loan to physically build the project. Has finite due date on which the loan will be replaced by a permanent, long-term loan.

GLOSSARY [continued]

Contingency The estimate for unknown or undetermined costs; a percentage of those unknown costs in question; not the known costs, such as land.

Contract of Sale Unrecorded; no formal title transfer. Seldom used anymore.

CPI Consumer Price Index

Design Review Commission [DRC] Public citizens, technically educated in design matters [usually], appointed by a City or County to decide upon matters of design. Sometimes called Architectural Review Commission [ARC].

Developer A party who organizes the process of a real estate project; purchasing the land and determining its use by researching the market, obtaining entitlements of use, designing the structure, obtaining financing, awarding contracts to build, and managing and/or selling the completed property[with an assist from Marvin T. Levin, author and attorney]. That's a developer!

Development Agreement Public agency contract with developer; usually for redevelopment project where agency wants something - i.e., park land dedication, school site, etc.

Discounted Cash Flow Computation of the future income stream in terms of present value, based upon the time value of money.

"Drop Dead" Date Last date for delivery of the premises, completion of the agreement, etc., after which there is no more "deal".

DSC or DSR Debt service coverage ratio; the ratio of the computed net income available to pay the mortgage divided by the mortgage payments. Usually a ratio of 1.10 to 1.30; used as a criterion in determining the loan amount.

EIR Environmental Impact Report.

Estoppel Statement Executed by lessee in favor of lessor; noting the acceptance of the premises, amount of rent, commencement date, defaults, if any, etc. Should be obtained for all projects, but an absolute requirement in refinancing.

Exactions Fees paid and land dedications made at the time development permits are issued.

Experience Curve The theorem, derived from manufacturing experience in World War II is: there is a 20-30% increase in productivity/decrease in cost during each time the number of repetitions is doubled. The base originates from zero experience.

Fair Market Value The cash [or equivalent] price for which a property will sell after reasonable exposure, without duress, and in a competitive market with a prudent buyer and seller. NOTE: The exact legal definition is longer; this is the gist.

Fannie Mae Federal National Mortgage Association is the nation's largest provider of residential mortgage funds. Primary function is to provide secondary market facilities for residential mortgages. Provides stability to this market by buying, selling and guaranteeing mortgages.

F.A.R. Floor Area Ratio; ratio of total building area to land area

GLOSSARY [continued]

Feasibility Study   Marketability study <u>plus</u> economic/cost analysis

FF&E   Fixtures, Furnishings and Equipment

Final Map   For major subdivisions. Creates the final entitlement to begin physical construction of the subdivision. Unless a "vesting tentative map", has finite completion date.

Focused EIR   Not a "full blown" EIR. Addresses <u>specific</u> issues such as noise, traffic, air pollution, etc.; limited number of environmental concerns.

Footprint   The building outline, in plan, on the site

Freddie Mac   Federal Home Loan Mortgage Corp.; secondary market in residential real estate loans where there are no guarantees a la Ginnie Mae/Fannie Mae.

General Plan   Long range [20 year "horizon"; approximately 5 year update to "track"]. Comprehensive document prepared by City/County planning agency to guide the physical development of that sphere of influence. A general plan shall include at least a circulation, conservation, housing, land use, noise, open-space, and safety element by State law.

Ginnie Mae   Government National Mortgage Association. Mortgage loans which are FHA insured or VA guaranteed. Creates secondary market. See Fannie Mae and Freddie Mac.

Hard Costs   The cost of the "sticks and stones" of a project. Sometimes includes design fees, permits, etc., and sometimes not.

HDCP   Handicapped [codes and requirements].

Highest and Best Use   Study to determine which physically or reasonably possible, appropriately supportive, financially feasible, and legally permissible use results in the highest land [development] value. <u>Not a marketability study</u>.

HVAC   Heating, Ventilating, and Air Conditioning

Incubator Space   Small industrial space; approximately 1,500 sq. ft. or less.

Initial Study   The preliminary analysis by the planning staff to determine possible environmental effects and concerns of the project. Basis for determining whether or not an EIR is required.

Insuring Party   The party responsible for <u>obtaining</u> the insurance, not necessarily paying for it.

Inventory   The amount of space or number of units available for a particular building type.

IRR   Internal Rate of Return; see Discounted Cash Flow.

Judicial Foreclosure   A foreclosure of a mortgage or lien by [legal] action rather than by a trustee sale.

JV   Joint Venture

LAFCO   Local Agency Formation Commission; responsible for city incorporation approvals and annexations.

Lead Agency   The ultimate responsible party, <u>usually</u> a City or County which has EIR's prepared, makes recommendations, is responsible for updating the general plan, etc.

LIBOR   London Inter Bank Offered Rate. Financing index coming into acceptance as financing becomes more global in scope.

GLOSSARY [continued]

Liquidated Damages Stipulated amount where damages cannot be ascertained, although this may be difficult to claim for income producing property, as the NOI already is projected. Cannot be in the form of a penalty, which is unenforceable in California.

Loan Constant The [percentage] multiplier of the loan amount to determine the annual loan payment; e.g., $1,000 loan @ 12% for 30 years has monthly payments of $10.29, the constant is 12.35 [annual payments of $123.48].

Lot Consolidation Combining two or more adjoining separate parcels into one lot.

LTV Loan To [appraised or economic] Value; ratio usually 70-80%.

MAI Appraisal "Member Appraisal Institute", not as sometimes referred to: "made as instructed"

Market Analysis Analysis projections regarding the components of demand for a particular type of space.

Market Knowledge The combination of the market study and market analysis plus experience as to the depth, breadth, and seasoning of the market.

Market Study Analysis projections regarding the supply of space available.

Marketability Study Determines the ability of the market to absorb space within a specific time, without considering economic viability.

Marketing Research The systematic gathering, recording, and analyzing of data about problems relating to the marketing of goods to guide clients.

Mortagee Person to whom property is mortgaged; the lender

Mortgagor Person who mortgages property; the borrower

Negative Declaration A "positive" statement in reality; that there are no significant environmental effects or concerns for a particular project.

Net-Net-Net Lease terminology meaning property taxes, maintenance, and insurance costs are borne by the lessee. Also written as "NNN".

NOI Net Operating Income. Gross income less [projected] vacancy and operating expenses.

Non-Recourse Financing The land and/or improvements are the sole collateral for the lender without recourse to the borrower for any deficiencies in the event of foreclosure. Recourse financing is seldom used; absent fraud, until recently never went after deficiency judgment; California being a "single cause" state.

Notice of Completion The legal document to be recorded ASAP after issuance of the Certificate of Occupancy [CofO]. This filing date establishes the period of time during which liens may be filed; 30 days for sub-contractors; 60 days for general contractors.

Parcel Map Technically, for minor subdivisions only. Sometimes used [in error] to describe tentative maps.

Permanent Financing aka "takeout" financing. The loan which is funded upon physical completion of the project and [usually] upon obtaining a pre-agreed level of occupancy and/or income. The typical home mortgage is a permanent loan.

GLOSSARY [continued]

Planning Commission [PC]   Public citizens, usually interested lay people, appointed by a City or County to decide upon matters of planning and zoning.

Planning Staff   The paid employees of a City or County's Planning Department

Points   Points are the loan origination fee which a lender charges, expressed as a percentage of the loan amount; a 2% fee is "2 points".

Pre-Payment Penalty   aka pre-payment "privilege". A stipulated amount or percentage to discourage early repayment of the principal loan balance, e.g., when interest rates are dropping and a high rate loan is in place. Applies mostly to permanent loans.

Procuring Cause   For brokerage commissions earned; the agent/broker who first procures a ready, willing, and able buyer [or lessee] for the agreed-upon price and terms. NOTE: The legal definition is quite lengthy, but this is the gist.

Proforma Analysis   A financial, preliminary cost analysis of the total project cost, not just the construction estimate or bids.

Purchase Money Mortgage   Non-recourse, and rare in California currently. Mortgage given to seller as part of the purchase price when buying property. It also may be a mortgage given to a third party, that makes a loan to the buyer, of real property to be used as part of dwelling, not more than four units occupied all or in part by buyer.

Punch List   The final inspection list for the project. Derivation of "punch" unknown...maybe as in "punch your light out" if not completed.

PV   Present value [or Puerto Vallarta, if you like Mexico!]

REO   Real Estate Owned [by lender]; foreclosed property.

Residual Value   Annual net income divided by [appropriate] cap rate less project's total cost. May be viewed as the "value added".

Schematic Drawings   The preliminary plans necessary for the form and definition of a project; includes site plan [building "footprint"], floor plan, elevations, and landscaping details [for use permit].

Soft Costs   "Indirect" costs, such as brokerage commissions, financing points and interest, etc. Most lenders' analyses include design fees, permit costs, etc. in this category, and not as "hard" costs.

Spec Building   Developed on speculation without a pre-existing tenant or buyer. Rare, at present, for commercial projects.

Starker Exchange   Tax-deferred exchange of property under section 1031 of the Federal Tax Code

Sub-Divisions: Major   Five [5] lots or more

Sub-Divisions: Minor   Four [4] lots or less; also called "lot split"

Subject To's   Conditions which are "subject to" the original loan which is being assumed

Subordination   Placing legal rights for recovery of one behind those of another, e.g., 2nd trust deed behind a 1st; property owner, not having full payment for land by developer, places land rights behind developer's construction loan.

GLOSSARY [continued]

Subrogation Waiver   Waives claim of substitution and recovery under insurance policy of another.

Takeout Financing   "Takes out" the construction lender from the construction loan. See Permanent Financing.

Tentative Map   For major subdivisions. Creates the real, intrinsic value when approved. May be the vehicle by which land is financed, although the physical construction [usually] cannot start. Has time limitation to record the Final Map.

TI's   Tenant Improvements

Turnkey Project   See "build-to-suit"

Value Added   See "residual value". May also include intangibles as flexibility in design, quality and appearance, ease in identification. Thought through and understood with the end user in mind.

Variance   Relatively minor "adjustments" in zoning requirements, setbacks, encroachments, and the like. Must be "unusual and special" to the particular property, and not merely because neighbor received a variance.

Vesting Tentative Map   A tentative sub-division map which, for all practical purposes, is valid for a definite length of time.

Working Drawings   The complete set of plans [civil/grading, architectural, structural, landscaping, mechanical, and electrical - if required] for the building permit application/approval and the bidding process.

Wrap Loan   Creates a new loan, and not necessarily with a formal institution [as in seller carry-back], and leaves existing loan in place. May have legal complications such as with a "due on sale" loan clause. Also called "piggyback".

Zoning Administrator [ZA]   While the ZA usually is the only member of a planning staff who has the power of approval or disapproval, some ordinances allow the Planning Director or Community Development Director to approve Conditional Use Permits or other similar types of permits.

Making the Deal Work

MAKING DEAL

INTRODUCTION

This section resumes where "Project Feasibility" finishes and might be subtitled "Legal Aspects......Keeping It Simple!". We shall cover what needs to happen <u>after</u> a project is determined to be a "go" and serious money needs to be committed.

Buying or "Controlling" the Property
Selecting the Design Consultants
Awarding the Construction Contract(s)
Managing the Construction
Negotiating With Users or Buyers

A basic assumption for this text's focus is that the permit processing....entitlement to use....is well in hand. And a reality of the focus is that, at times, all items will be on the "critical path". The purpose of this text will be to understand how to juggle all of these balls at the same time without dropping them or losing your sanity!

An underlying theme for each of the topics herein, is that all of the participants in the development....architects, engineers, contractors and vendors, construction and property managers...**will be compensated reasonably and fairly for their efforts** - maybe even with incentives - **and paid in a timely manner.**

Another theme is to **understand the necessary ingredients for clear and concise design or construction contracts, written with the intention of defining performance and resolving conflicts in a reasonable manner.**

The American Institute of Architects (A.I.A) publishes various contract forms for architectural and construction work, including construction general conditions (A201). These contract forms are used widely, yet are flawed in several ways. Generally, they favor the architect first, then the owner, and lastly, the general contractor. The documents of 1974 thru 1986 virtually made the
architect judge and jury, with many provisions providing ample cause for litigation to gain reasonable solutions for <u>either</u> the owner or contractor, or both. The A.I.A revised their documents in 1987. They are better than before, but still have a strong bias toward the architect. If you are presented with prior versions, ask why they are not using the 1987 version.

NOTE: The A.I.A. began revising all of their documents in 1997. Final revisions and printing thereof were accomplished in Spring, 1998. Such documents have not been reviewed by the author.

The Associated General Contractors (A.G.C.) also publishes construction contracts and the attendant general conditions. A.G.C. documents, generally, are less widely used than the A.I.A. forms, and tend to favor the general contractor (although less obviously than the A.I.A. favors the architect), with the owner still in 2nd place.

And of course you can prepare your own design and construction documents from scratch...potentially a tedious, time consuming and (often) expensive process. You will be better off (usually) utilizing the "standard" documents with which most parties are familiar, and modifying them to clarify and protect your own best interests in an appropriate manner.

NOTE: The following subject matter is intended as general information only, and is <u>not</u> <u>intended as legal advice</u>. For a specific property acquisition, this may be used as a topical guide in concert with <u>knowledgeable, competent and appropriate counsel</u> for anything which may affect a particular legal position or entitlement.

P U R C H A S E   A G R E E M E N T

On behalf of _____, this Offer to Purchase is submitted, subject to the following:

1.   <u>LOCATION</u>
     That certain parcel of land designated and/or commonly known as _____
     _____and having Assessor's Parcel No._____, containing
     a total area of _____, per the attached Exhibit "A". A complete legal
     description shall be furnished in escrow by Seller.

2.   <u>PRELIMINARY TITLE REPORT</u>
     Buyer agrees to approve or disapprove the preliminary title report within ten (10) working days after it has been presented to Buyer by Seller through the escrow office. Seller shall have forty-five (45) calendar days to cure any title defects which Buyer may disapprove.

3.   <u>PARCEL MAP/ENGINEERING DATA</u>
     Buyer understands that the parcel to be conveyed is a legal lot, filed under a recorded parcel map/subdivision map. The map shall be furnished to Buyer at the earliest possible time, at no additional cost. Any topographic maps, soils reports, utility or street improvement plans, and related items which presently may be in Seller's custody, similarly will be provided to Buyer at no additional cost.

4.   <u>USE PERMIT(S)</u>
     Prior to close of escrow, Buyer will have obtained the necessary use and building permits from _____ allowing occupancy of the premises within a _____ sq. ft. building, and for an intended use of _____._Such permit(s) shall include an appropriate environmental impact report with a negative declaration statement with respect to the development.

5.   <u>ASSESSMENTS</u>
     Buyer understands that, at present, there are no bonded assessments or other charges "running with the land". Seller hereby agrees to pay, prior to close of escrow, any such fees, liens, acreage fees, or related items, recorded or unrecorded, which are encumbrances or charges against the subject premises. This will enable Buyer to have free and clear title to the subject premises except for any recorded conditions, covenants, restrictions, and easements. Specifically excluded from this are fees for traffic signalization, school tax, fire districts, etc. which are paid as part of the building permit and are the responsibility of Buyer.

6.   <u>TITLE INSURANCE AND CLOSING COSTS</u>
     _____ shall pay for the title insurance policy. Seller shall pay for documentary stamps and any "special" _____ County taxes or fees not otherwise included as fees for the use and/or building permits. The balance of the escrow costs shall be borne by Buyer and Seller, in their respective shares, consistent with existing _____ County practice and custom.

                                   Page 1 of 3

7. REAL ESTATE BROKERAGE COMMISSIONS
    Any real estate brokerage commissions which may be due from the sale of the subject premises shall be the sole responsibility of Seller. Any real estate brokerage commissions which may be due from an executed lease on and for the subject premises which is executed by Buyer, shall be the sole responsibility of Buyer.

8. UTILITIES/IMPROVEMENTS
    Buyer understands that the developed site includes all utilities (gas, sewer, storm drainage, electrical, telephone, cable TV, and water), available at least to the property line, and that connections thereto would bear only the "normal" servicing/connections fees. Buyer further understands that required frontage improvements (curb, gutter, and sidewalk) are in place, that street paving sections are in conformance with _____requirements and that no further site development work is required except as follows:

9. PURCHASE PRICE
    _____ all cash to be paid at close of escrow.

10. ESCROW CLOSING
    The escrow will close within thirty (30) days upon issuance of the _____ permit by _____.

11. ESCROW OFFICE
    The escrow shall be opened within three (3) working days after receipt by Buyer of Seller's acceptance at:

12. ADDITIONAL ESCROW INSTRUCTIONS
    Buyer and Seller shall execute additional instructions which may be required by the escrow office and not be inconsistent with the provisions noted herein.

13. PRORATIONS
    Real property taxes, rentals, premiums on insurance accepted by Buyer, and other costs, if any, shall be prorated as of the date of recordation of the deed to Buyer.

14. ASSIGNMENT
    Buyer reserves the right to assign its rights and to be relieved of any future liability under this agreement, provided that the assignee shall assume all of the obligations of Buyer.

15. OWNERSHIP
    Title to the property, when taken by Buyer, shall be vested in the name of _____ _____ and/or its nominee. Should Buyer elect to effect a 1031 exchange pursuant to the Internal Revenue Code, such exchange shall be made at no additional expense or liability to Seller.

16. TIME
    Time is of the essence, and notification of Seller's response is required prior to 5:00 p.m., _____, or this agreement shall have no further force or effect.

Page 2 of 3

PURCHASE AGREEMENT (continued)

17. <u>SELLER'S EXECUTION</u>
Buyer's application for conditional use permits and related matters will require Seller's signature as the existing owner. Seller hereby agrees to execute such required documents in a timely manner and in the event of Seller's absence, provide a person, readily available, with Seller's power of attorney to execute such documents.

18. <u>ADDITIONAL PROVISIONS</u>

<u>Hazardous Waste Disclosure Statement</u> [pages 67 and 68]
<u>Liquidated Damages</u> [page 69] also for use in a Construction Contract
<u>Buyer As Broker</u> [page 69]
<u>Power of Attorney</u> if Seller is infirmed, divorcing or likely to be unavailable for an extended time
<u>Property In Probate or Foreclosure</u>?
<u>1031 Exchange [Starker]</u>

<u>Additional Consideration For Improved Property</u>

Structural Renovation?	Building Systems, Equipment
Verify Physical Condition	Other Structures On Property?
Conversion of Use	Technical and Service Manuals
Seller's Personnel Transfers	Personal Property To Remain
Service Contracts/Warranties	Income/Expense **[from tax returns]**
Lease Review, New Leases	Estoppel Statements

Due Diligence Inspections; especially Roofing, HVAC, Seismic

BUYER:

_____   Date:_____
Its

SELLER: Accepts the above terms and conditions this _____ day of _____.

By: _____

Address: _____

_____

Telephone: _____

ENVIRONMENTAL QUESTIONNAIRE AND DISCLOSURE STATEMENT

PROPERTY LOCATION: Set Forth On <u>Exhibit "A"</u> Hereto (the "Property").

1.   <u>Current And Former Uses Of The Property</u>.

        (a)   Please name the current and all former owners of the Property.

        (b)   Describe all current uses of the Property. (If other than office use exclusively, please provide the names of all current occupants and dates of occupancy.)

        (c)   What is the date of completion of original construction and any substantial renovations (including tenant improvements)?

        (d)   Please name all previous occupants of the Property.

        (e)   Describe all previous uses of the Property.

        (f)   Describe all uses of properties adjacent to the Property.

2.   <u>Asbestos</u>.

        (a)   Is there asbestos currently in any of the construction materials contained in the buildings at the Property?

        (b)   If so, has a survey been conducted to assess the type, amount, location and condition of asbestos? (Please attach a copy of any survey report.)

        (c)   Have asbestos air samples been taken? If so, what are the results?

3.   <u>Polychlorinated Biphenyls ("PCBs")</u>.

        (a)   Have "PCBs" been used in electrical transformers, capacitors or other equipment located at the Property?

        (b)   If so, please describe the nature of use and quantity of PCBs used at the Property.

4.   <u>Storage Tanks, Drums And Pipelines</u>.

        (a)   Are there now or have there been any above-ground or underground gasoline, diesel, crude oil, gas, or other chemical storage tanks on the Property? If so, please describe all of the substances stored in the tanks, the capacity of such tanks, and (if removed or closed), the date and compliance with tank closure laws of such removal or closure.

        (b)   Have the tanks been inspected or tested for leakage? If so, when was the most recent test and what were the results of the test?

        (c)   Are any other chemicals stored on the Property in drums or other containers? If so, please describe the substances, the quantities stored and the type of containers.

        (d)   Are there now or have there been any pipelines to, from or across all or any of the Property, or any easements or rights of way therefor? If so, please describe all such pipelines, the owners or operators thereof, and the rights of way materials carried in such pipelines.

        (e)   Have there been any spills, leaks or other releases or chemicals on the Property? If so, please describe the chemicals and the quantities thereof released, all cleanup measures taken and the results of any soil or groundwater samples performed to detect the presence of the chemicals spilled, leaked or released on the Property.

        (f)   Please attach copies of any and all permits or licenses pertaining to the use, storage, handling or disposal of chemicals or to the use and maintenance of any above-ground or underground tanks or pipelines on the Property.

5.   <u>Air Emissions</u>.

        (a)   Describe all air emissions from each source of air pollutants, including fuel burning equipment (describing the type of fuel burned), on the Property.

        (b)   Describe all air pollution control equipment used to reduce emissions for each source of air emissions.

        (c)   Are air emissions monitored? If so, what is the frequency of such monitoring?

        (d)   Please attach copies of any and all air permits or licenses pertaining to operations on the Property.

6.   <u>Water Discharges From The Property</u>.

        (a)   List all sources of waste water discharges to surface waters, septic systems or holding ponds.

        (b)   List all sources of waste-water discharges to public sewer systems.

        (c)   For each discharge, list the average daily flow.

        (d)   Please attach copies of any and all water discharge permits or licenses pertaining to operations on the Property.

7.   <u>Waste Disposal</u>.

        (a)   Describe the types of liquid wastes (other than waste-water described in part 6 above) and solid wastes generated at the Property.

        (b)   Describe how the liquid and solid wastes generated at the Property are disposed.

        (c)   Please attach copies of any and all waste disposal permits or licenses pertaining to operations on the Property.

PURCHASE AGREEMENT (continued)
ENVIRONMENTAL QUESTIONNAIRE AND DISCLOSURE STATEMENT (continued)

8.   If the Property Has Been Or Is Currently Used For Industrial Purposes, Please Provide The Following Additional Information.

(a)   Has the Property been used for the disposal of any liquid or solid waste? If so, please describe the location of all disposal sites, the type(s) of wastes disposed at each site, the results of any soil or groundwater samples taken in the vicinity of each site and the manner in which each site not presently in use was closed.

(b)   Have evaporation or storage ponds ever been located on the Property? If so, please describe the location of all such ponds, the type(s) of wastes placed in each pond, the results of any soil or groundwater samples taken in the vicinity of each pond and the manner in which each pond not presently in use was closed.

(c)   Have waste-water treatment facilities, such as acid neutralization vaults, ever been located on the Property? If so, please describe the location of all such facilities, the type(s) of products or wastes stored in each facility, the amount(s) of products or wastes stored in each facility, the results of any soil or groundwater samples taken in the vicinity of each facility and the manner in which each facility not presently in use was closed.

9.   If The Property Has Been Or Is Currently Used For Agricultural Purposes, Please Provide The Following Additional Information.

(a)   Have pesticides, herbicides or other agricultural chemicals been applied to the Property? If so, please describe the location(s) where such pesticides, herbicides or chemicals were applied in each area and the results of any soil or groundwater analyses performed to detect pesticides, herbicides or chemicals used at the Property.

(b)   Have pesticides, herbicides or other agricultural chemicals been mixed, formulated, rinsed or disposed of on the Property? If so, please describe the location(s) where such pesticides, herbicides or chemicals were mixed, formulated, rinsed or disposed, the type(s) of pesticides, herbicides or chemicals mixed, formulated, rinsed or disposed of at each location, and the results of any soil or groundwater analyses performed to detect pesticides, herbicides or chemicals mixed, formulated, rinsed or disposed of at the Property.

10.   If Any Fill Has Been Deposited On Or Occurred On The Property, Please Provide The Following Additional Information.

(a)   Have the constituents of such fill been analyzed, tested and monitored? If so, please furnish the results of such testing and monitoring.

(b)   Are any hazardous or toxic materials known or believed to exist in any such fill constituents?

11.   Lead-Based Paint **[To be completed only if the Property presently is or will be improved with one or more residential dwellings (including apartment units) which were constructed prior to 1978.]**

(a)   Has the Property been found to be lead-based paint free by an inspector certified under the federal certification program or under a federally accredited state or tribal certification program? If yes, please attach a copy of such certified inspector's report.

(b)   Does the Property contain lead-based paint or lead-based paint hazards including any condition that causes exposure to lead from lead-contaminated dust, lead-contaminated soil, or lead-contaminated paint that is deteriorated or present in accessible surfaces, friction surfaces, or impact surfaces)? If yes, please give all additional information available concerning the known lead-based paint and/or lead-based paint hazards, such as the basis for the determination that lead-based paint and/or lead-based paint hazards exist, the location of the lead-based paint and/or lead-based paint hazards, and the condition of the painted surfaces.

(c)   List and please attach a copy of all available records and reports pertaining to lead-based paint and/or lead-based paint hazards in the Property that are in Borrower's possession or that are reasonably obtainable by Borrower. If no such records or reports are available, please so state.

As the present owner of the Property (or the duly authorized representative of such owner), the undersigned is familiar with all of the operations presently conducted on the Property, has made diligent inquiry into the former uses of the Property and hereby certifies to and for the benefit of Lender that to the best of its knowledge, information and belief the information disclosed above is true and correct.

Date: _____

BORROWER: _____

EXHIBIT "A":   LEGAL DESCRIPTION OF PROPERTY

Source: Karl E. Geier
                Miller, Starr & Regalia

PURCHASE AGREEMENT (continued)

LIQUIDATED DAMAGES [Buyer's/Contractor's Failure to Perform] If escrow does not close due to Buyer's default, then escrow shall be cancelled as provided above, but escrow holder is irrevocably instructed to deliver the deposits to Seller as liquidated damages for Buyer's failure to complete the purchase pursuant to California Civil Code Sections 1671, 1676, and 1677, it being acknowledged by Buyer and Seller that the damages which Seller would sustain would be impracticable or extremely difficult to fix or determine. Buyer and Seller agree that Seller's economic detriment resulting from the removal of the property from the real estate market, and other activities in furtherance of this agreement, would be extremely difficult to ascertain.

Accordingly, Buyer and Seller agree that the deposits required herein are a reasonable estimate of Seller's damages. Due to the special nature of negotiations which preceded acceptance by Seller of Buyer's offer to acquire the property, the parties acknowledge that the actual damages caused Seller by the failure to close escrow would be extremely difficult to establish. In addition, Buyer desires to have a limitation on his potential liability to Seller if this transaction fails to close. Therefore, in order to induce Seller to waive all other remedies Seller may have in the event of breach by Buyer of his obligations hereunder, Buyer and Seller have agreed to the concept of liquidated damages as set forth herein, with the amount and timing of the payment having been the subject of negotiations between the parties. In addition, Buyer shall pay all title and escrow cancellation charges. By placing their initials below, Buyer and Seller acknowledge that they have read, understood, and agreed to be bound by this liquidated damages provision.

NOTE: For Construction contract[s], references to "escrow", "property" etc. will be deleted, and "project", "revenue", etc. will be added

BUYER IS BROKER [if applicable]
Buyer hereby discloses that one of its principals [partners, etc.], _____
_____, is a licensed real estate broker in the State of California. Buyer further discloses that Buyer is purchasing the property described herein on Buyer's own behalf as a principal.
Neither, Buyer, _____[Broker]_____ nor any affiliate, employer, or employee of Buyer is taking a commission or receiving any other compensation in connection with this purchase transaction. Buyer and Seller hereby agree and acknowledge that Buyer and [Broker] are not acting as a broker in this transaction, and Seller understands that, if Buyer or [Broker] were acting as an agent of Seller, Buyer or [Broker] might have a duty to disclose to Seller all material facts relating to Buyer's decisions to purchase the property. Seller further understands that Buyer and [Broker] are not in any way acting as an agent of the Seller. Buyer and Seller hereby agree and acknowledge that Buyer and [Broker] make no representations to Seller regarding any aspect of this transaction, except as are set forth in this Agreement.

NOTE: Provisions for liquidated damages always should be included in option agreements

REQUEST NO._____

DATE_____

PAYMENT REQUEST AND RELEASE OF LIEN

Request is hereby made to _____
_____ for payment of \$_____ which represents labor and materials furnished to _____ for the construction of improvements on that project known as _____. In consideration of and as an inducement to make the payment the undersigned certifies and agrees that the work, labor or materials have been actually performed or furnished; that all bills for work, labor and material to and including the date of said order have been paid; that the undersigned will hold the owners, the general contractor and _____
_____ harmless of and from any claims or demands for work, labor and materials furnished or performed by or for the account of the undersigned to and including the date of said order; and the undersigned does hereby waive in favor of the owners, the general contractor, and _____
_____ any lien which it might otherwise have for any such work, labor or materials furnished or performed to and including the date of said order; and the undersigned further agrees that any lien to which it may be entitled against the property upon which said work is being performed at any time shall be subject and subordinate to the lien or charge of the Deed of Trust held by _____. It is understood that this release is to be effective upon actual receipt of and negotiation of a check for payment of the heretofore named account.

_____

By _____

APPROVED:

Its _____

_____

CONTRACTOR/OWNER

ENDORSEMENT OF CHECK*

DO NOT SIGN IN THIS SPACE
Endorse in Space Below

To induce payment of this check:
Each Payee certifies and warrants that all work, labor or materials to the date indicated on the face of this check have been actually performed or furnished and that all materials and labor furnished were paid for in cash.
Payee(s) covenants to save and hold _____ harmless from any claims for labor or materials which may be asserted or demanded by any suppliers or laborers, or their assigns, on account of labor or materials furnished prior to the date indicated on the face of this check.
By the endorsement of this check, Payee(s) hereby fully releases and waives all mechanics' lien and equitable lien rights, stop notice rights, and any other claims, demands and actions known or unknown of any type of kind arising out of or related to the work furnished to the date and on the job address referred to on the face of this check.

_____

_____

OFFICIAL ENDORSEMENT REQUIRED
(MUST BE SIGNED PERSONALLY AND MUST
STATE AUTHORITY - PRES., OWNER, ETC.)

* Often used as rubber stamp on back of check

MAKING DEAL

"Quality is not an act, it is a habit" - **Aristotle**

INTERFACING WITH YOUR CONSULTANTS

GETTING STARTED; QUESTIONS - DEVELOPER to CONSULTANT; CONSULTANT to DEVELOPER
What is the specific purpose of the project? What activities will it house?
Has a site been selected?
Has a construction budget and/or schedule been established?
What are design aspirations? [read in quality and/or cost]
What are **your** overall expectations or objectives from the project?
How will decisions be made....individually or by committee? [relates to **both** consultant and
   developer]. How much detail is required?
Is the project experimental? Is technology pushed to the limit or merely limited?
How much experience does each party have in the process?

SELECTING THE ARCHITECT [A.I.A. Guidelines]
When should the architect be retained? A. As early as possible
Look at more than one firm? A. Yes, assuming a good relationship does not already exist.
How to determine firms to contact? A. From owners who have developed similar facilities;
   designers of buildings which you like
Information to request from interview? Type of interview? Formal or casual
How many firms to interview?
Basis of decision? Who works on job; compatability of work styles
Select builder/contractor before selecting architect?

SELECTION IS A MUTUAL PROCESS!

IDENTIFY SERVICES WHICH YOU NEED
 * Pre-design Services
** Site Analysis Services
   Schematic Design/Design Development Services
   Construction Documents/Bidding or Negotiation Services
   Construction Contract Administration Services
   Post Construction Services
   Supplemental Services: Renderings, Model Construction, Life Cycle Cost Analysis
     Energy Studies, Tenant Services, Graphics Design, Fine Arts/Special
     Furnishings, Promotion/Public Relations, Leasing Brochure,
     Computer Applications, Materials Testing, Special Presentation- Video,
     Photography, etc.

  * Permits, Feasibility, Pre-leasing
 ** Soils, Toxics, etc.

"CALIFORNIA CONSTRUCTION LAW"; May, 1991; p. 96
If the architect's mistake does not arise from negligence or intentional misconduct, the extra
construction cost and time will have to be absorbed by the owner.

INTERFACING WITH YOUR CONSULTANTS [continued]

TIPS:
1. Clearly analyze and define the scope of work to be performed, and the time in which it is to be accomplished, <u>including</u> time at agency/commission meetings
2. Agree on payment schedule; flat rate or hourly fee, **not a % of cost**
3. Do as much as you can yourself....legwork, documents, copies, etc.
4. Meet in **their** office if much travel time involved
5. Clarify what is included in fee - i.e. automobile mileage, telephone, copies, blueprinting [maximum?], etc.
6. [Some] Structural engineers can do entire project?...especially if "simple" as an industrial project
7. Pay bills in a timely manner, or let consultant know **when** the bills will be paid
8. Rights for reproduction of prints? Usually Architect/Engineer retain ownership [rights] of the drawings
9. If A.I.A. standard form, read very, very carefully (see Preface regarding new 1998 documents)

BASIC ELEMENTS OF THE OWNER - ARCHITECT AGREEMENT

Scope of Work
a. Preliminary or Conceptual Plans (approval by Owner)
b. Schematic Drawings
c. Working Drawings and Specifications
d. Time Frame to Complete a., b., and c.
e. Inspections during construction? Frequency?
f. Change Order approval, administration and negotiation. How much involvement with this by the Owner? How knowledgeable is the Owner? Or the Architect?
g. Project Wrap-up and completion of the "Punch List"

Budget and Bidding Process
Generally, **do not rely on the Architect for much other than cursory budgeting work.** It will be rare if the Architect has <u>accurate</u> cost records from past projects. For <u>accurate</u>, pre-bidding cost estimates, there are consulting cost estimating firms which can provide quality service, primary of which is the Saylor Consulting Group, San Francisco (see Source Reference Material). Up to $3,000 with schematic drawings.

Become actively involved in the bidding process, and <u>carefully</u> consider negotiated construction contracts (which are consistent with estimates noted above) rather than a sealed bid opening with several contractors.

Fees
a. Hourly or Fixed Fee as appropriate
b. Segregation of hourly rates for: principal, associate architect, drafting or C.A.D. design, and clerical
c. Fees to include "usual and customary" overhead charges: Copies, telephone, automobile mileage, etc.
   NOTE: some architects bill separately for these costs, which irritates many clients

INTERFACING WITH YOUR CONSULTANTS (continued)

BASIC ELEMENTS OF THE OWNER - ARCHITECT AGREEMENT (continued)

Fees (continued)

d.   Typically, the Architect contracts directly with Civil/Structural Engineers, Mechanical/Electrical Engineers and Landscape Architects for their services, adding a markup to these additional consulting costs. Consider paying the consultants directly, avoiding the additional cost. Architects will say they "lose control", but this is a specious argument, in my opinion.

e.   **<u>Never, never, never</u> have a design contract which has payment based upon a percentage of the construction cost.** The reasons are obvious: (a) no <u>real</u> incentive for the design team to save money, and (b) a simple change in fixturization, hardware or interior finishes can reduce a project's cost by tens of thousands of dollars, thereby reducing the fee without any <u>real</u> reduction of time and effort. Back to the fundamental principle: reasonable pay for the work performed

Ownership of Drawings; Printing

Generally, the Architect (and the other design consultants) retain possession and ownership of the original tracings. Printing of the construction drawings can be a large cost if the project is complicated in scope, and has many sub-contractors.   Include a specified number of <u>full set</u> construction drawings to be furnished by the architect in your basic contract.   For additional sets, changes orders, etc., clarify in the contract how these are to be handled - i.e. reproduceables to the owner for their printing cost <u>or</u> architect provides <u>at cost</u> without markup.

Change Order Approval, Administration and Negotiation

This condenses to how much involvement the owner wishes to assume. For larger projects, a construction manager may perform this function. Perhaps an "as needed" consultant can assist. The point is to think clearly through this process as to what best meets your "comfort zone".....You are not <u>mandated by law</u> to have the architect handle change order tasks, merely because it says so in the A.I.A document!

Insurance

For professional liability coverage, insurance is offered on a "claims-made" basis, or with the more expensive "project-specific" coverage. Usual and customary coverage is "claims-made". <u>This coverage applies only as long as the</u> <u>policy is in force.</u> Further, there may be a significant deductible; generally, though it's $5-10,000.

Decisions

Rendering a decision within a "reasonable time" is understood to mean no more than two (2) weeks....14 <u>calendar</u> days.

REMEMBER: THERE NEVER HAS BEEN A PERFECT AGREEMENT. However, including these elements, and questioning everything which you do not understand clearly or don't feel comfortable about, eliminates much of the potential problems in the development process.

STANDARD PROVISIONS OF AGREEMENT
BETWEEN CLIENT AND CONSULTANT

This Form B Agreement, © 1998, was developed by the Consulting Engineers and Land Surveyors of California (CELSOC). It is the equivalent of the scope in the General Conditions published by the American Institute of Architects (AIA) and the Associated General Contractors (AGC) for their membership. However, it is *relatively* impartial, and generally clarifies, rather than favors the initiating party (Consultant).

Following are important paraphrased excerpts and commentary concerning the Agreement:

Ownership of Drawings All reports, plans, specifications, notes, electronic media documents prepared by Consultant are instruments of service, and shall remain the property of Consultant.

Document Conflicts In the event of a conflict between the signed construction documents prepared by Consultant and electronic files, the signed/stamped hard copy construction documents shall govern. Client agrees to require its contractor and subcontractors to *review all construction documents* prior to the commencement of construction-phase work. Any deficiencies shall be noted promptly so they may be corrected by Consultant prior to commencement of construction-phase work.

Construction Services Inclusion (or waiver) of construction-phase services to be performed by Consultant.
Very important for Consultant to participate in this phase.

Lender Indemnity Client acknowledges that field and other conditions may change by the time project construction occurs. Clarifications, adjustments and modifications resulting therefrom shall be paid for by Client as extra services.
Client acknowledges that any unauthorized changes and their effects are not the responsibility of Consultant. Client agrees to indemnify and hold Consultant harmless from all claims and costs arising from such unauthorized changes.

Cost Estimates/Budget Consultant's estimates of probable construction costs do not constitute representations, warranties or guarantees of such opinions, as compared to bid or actual costs.

Limited Liability Client agrees to limit the liability of Consultant for any claim or action arising in tort, contract or strict liability to $50,000 or Consultant's fee, whichever is greater.
This clause to be initialed. Amount may be negotiated upward for a very large project or to limits of Consultant's insurance. Has been upheld in California courts - see Markbourough case.

Hazardous Waste Excludes any services by Consultant related in any way to asbestos, lead or toxic materials.

Litigation Venue for any litigation brought to enforce provisions of this Agreement will be brought and adjudicated in the county in which Consultant's place of business is located.
Client may want to change this.

Arbitration Any disputes relating to this Agreement shall first be submitted to (non-binding) mediation. Failing to resolve the dispute with mediation, the matter shall be submitted to binding arbitration in accordance with the Construction Industry Rules of the American Arbitration Association. *Client and Consultant agree to include a similar clause with all of their separate independent and general contractors, subcontractors, consultants, suppliers and fabricators.*
The foregoing litigation clause and this clause are contradictory, and one or the other should be deleted. Mediation/arbitration is recommended, but be sure that all parties involved have a similar clause.

Condominium Projects

- Client does not now foresee that this project will be converted into a condominium (if such be the case)
  Conversion affects the design and consultant's work
- Client acknowledges the risk to Consultant inherent in condominium projects
- Client agrees to indemnify and hold Consultant harmless from all claims, liabilities, costs, etc. arising from this Agreement, negligence or willful misconduct excepted
  Many Design Professionals no longer will work on condominium projects. And many insurance companies will not provide professional liability coverage
- Client agrees that the bylaws of the Homeowner's Association contain a requirement that all inspections recommended in the Maintenance Manual have been performed. Further, all necessary maintenance has been performed as a result of these inspections
- Appropriate waiver and indemnity in favor of Client, Consultant(s), Contractor, etc. if the maintenance recommendations are not performed

General Notes

- *Be aware that all parties will be sued or subject to mediation/arbitration costs in the event of a dispute. The goal of a good agreement (and well run project) is to have appropriate parties dismissed from the proceedings as quickly as possible with a minimum expenditure of time and money*
- *Re: ownership of drawings, the Consultant's work is a service, not a product. Product liability laws impose a much stricter standard of care on the Consultant and do not require proof of negligence*
- *If for some reason Client insists on ownership of the drawings, the matter should be reviewed with counsel as liability therefrom may shift between Client and Consultant*
- *With ownership of the drawings, Consultant may use the drawings again on another project, such as a "cookie cutter". Although rare, this matter should be clarified to avoid possible future disputes*
- *Other "related costs" in litigation or arbitration clauses should include arbitration fees for "expert witnesses"*

MAKING DEAL

SELECTING [and Meshing With] YOUR CONTRACTOR

CONSIDER IN SELECTION PROCESS:
1. Contractor not a partner [usually], but don't make an adversary either
2. Probably more time spent with contractor than anyone else
3. Contractor may have more impact on job than anyone else......can alienate prospects, potential clients
4. Friendships lost by using "friends"....at least initially
5. Considerations

Prior Work	Current Work Load (manpower;
Recommendations/Referrals	25% of last year's volume?)
Compatability [esp. remodels]	Union/Non-Union
Do It Now If Possible	Inclement Weather Work
"Change Order Artist"?	Attitude With Consultants

NOTE: Develop "us-us", not "us-them" relationship

TYPE OF CONTRACT:
Cost Plus Fixed Fee, incl. Supervision.
Lump Sum
Time and Materials [T&M]; least desirable. Remodels? To a maximum?
Owner as "General" - Separate Contracts; least costly; can be most efficient

   For each of the above: [a] define change order labor rates; [b] owner assumes warranty call back responsibility?

PRELIMINARY BUDGET:
1. Begin as soon as building "footprint" known
2. Define who gathers what costs - i.e. permits, off-site, etc.
3. Understand the general and technical specifications; and know what you are supposed to be getting
4. Cost breakdown/quantity takeoff
5. Coordination with Architect - all information available?
6. Design and build? HVAC, Electrical, Plumbing. Consultant to inspect.
7. Agree on where to cut corners; understand about deferred maintenance items

DEVELOPER/CONTRACTOR RESPONSIBILITIES
DEVELOPER: Public hearings, A&E fees, permit fees, initial survey and staking, soils report, financing/leasing brochure, broker/marketing contacts

CONTRACTOR: Construction contract[?], lender cost breakdown schedule, permit revisions, knowledge of Codes, preliminary/final estimates

   NOTE: Contractor must be able to provide quick estimates for change orders; may have to make a decision in field on the spot

SELECTING [and Meshing With] YOUR CONTRACTOR [continued]

FINAL COST ESTIMATE:
1. Over budget - where to reduce? Look for where the <u>real money</u> is. May have earlier maintenance
2. Bidding coverage, without saturation
3. Bid too low
4. Uninsured contractors [or consultants]; be aware of potential problems
5. To whom bid? If direct to owner, keep contractor advised of costs
6. Agreement on scope of work and time schedule
7. Contract award; break ground

FAST TRACK SCHEDULING:
Some risk as not all costs precisely determined. Generally for larger, phased projects or those with substantial grading

DURING CONSTRUCTION:
1. Be on the job; be accessible
2. Schedule A&E inspections
3. Meet with building inspectors. Can do without getting in the way
4. Ask questions. Notice details. Speak up if something doesn't look right

POTENTIAL PROBLEM AREAS:
1. Client to Contractor - never lose control of client. Scheduling of client's fixturizations, improvements
2. Codes, material testing
3. Inspections - A&E
4. Slow payments (by owner or by contractor to sub-contractors)
5. Change order documentation
6. ***Should Contractor "Have Known"?**
7. Prompt call backs; completion of "punch list"
8. Lack of commonality of purpose between owner and contractor, since the ultimate interests of each are not necessarily identical

* <u>Manifestly Omitted Details Clause</u>
This clause holds the contractor responsible for items of work which are necessary for an acceptable final product but were inadvertently omitted by the contract documents. The theory is that it should have been obvious that this work was necessary to complete the project.

SELECTING [and Meshing With] YOUR CONTRACTOR (continued)
BID PACKAGE EXAMPLE

I INVITATION TO BID

ENSURE THAT "Invitation to Bid Documents" DO NOT INVALIDATE ANY PROVISIONS OF THE GENERAL CONDITIONS RE: CONTRACTOR'S RESPONSIBILITY FOR INSPECTION

Date _____

EASYWAY FOOD COMPANY
DESIGN AND CONSTRUCTION DEPARTMENT
200 MADISON STREET
MOUNTAINTOWN, WESTAMERICA 99999

Gentlemen:

Re: INVITATION TO BID
NO. 16

We are pleased to enclose one set of plans and specifications covering Site Earthwork and Fencing for the Dry Storage Warehouse to be constructed in Mountaintown, West America.

Bids will be received until 2:00 p.m., _____, at our main office at the above address. All bids shall be binding for 30 days thereafter. Bidders are invited to send one representative to a bid opening which will be conducted at the above specified time.

While we are asking all bidders to base their bids in accordance with the Owner's schedule, alternate completion dates will be given consideration based upon our evaluation of the advantages or disadvantages of the proposed schedule.

Attached hereto is the following information:
    1. Three copies each of our Bid Form.
    2. Two copies of the Construction Contract including Exhibit A and attachments listed therein.

Two copies of the executed Bid Form are to be submitted with your bid. All bids are requested to be itemized as noted on the Bid Form.

[1] If you are the successful bidder, it will be necessary for you to furnish a 100% Payment and Performance Bond in accordance with "The Standard Form of Bond" latest edition, copyrighted by the American Institute of Architects and issued by a Surety Company satisfactory to owner. You also will be expected to execute a contract in the form included with the attached documents.

[2] Owner reserves the right to reject any and all proposals or to waive irregularities noted therein. Owner reserves the right to evaluate each and every proposal in its absolute discretion and to accept any particular proposal even though the price or completion date, or both, may not be as favorable as some other proposal.

Bidders requesting additional information are advised to address their inquiries to Construction Management and Control, Inc., Attention: Mr. O. Hanson, telephone number (000) 123-4567.

[1]   See Appendix "C" for Special Report on Bonding   EASYWAY FOOD COMPANY
            (and Liquidated Damages)

[2]   The last sentence is used rather frequently. And   By Peter J. Cleaveland
            this may lead to (a) reduced number of bidders, or   Manager, Design and Construction Department
            (b) potential legal conflicts.

SELECTING [And Meshing With] YOUR CONTRACTOR (continued)

I I Bid Form (including Bid Breakdown)

Add: The Contractor and each Subcontractor shall evaluate and satisfy themselves as to the conditions and limitations under which the Work is to be performed, including without limitation:
- location, condition, layout and nature of the Project site and surroundings
- generally prevailing climatic conditions
- anticipated labor supply
- material availability
- other pertinent issues & details

NOTES:
Job site meeting held for general contractor and subcontractors.
One meeting or separate?
Bid results publicly announced?

Schedule of Values:
Line items of work
Separate Overhead and Profit categories
Scheduled rates for principal subcontractors for extra work/change orders
Requested alternates

BID FORM

DATE _____
INVITATION TO BID: 16
SITE EARTHWORK AND FENCING
DRY STORAGE WAREHOUSE
MOUNTAINTOWN, WEST AMERICA

TO: EASYWAY FOOD COMPANY
      Design and Construction Department
      200 Madison Street
      Mountaintown, West America 99999

Gentlemen:

Having examined the contract drawings, specifications and addenda nos. _____, and having examined and familiarized ourselves with the on-site conditions, the undersigned hereby does tender the following bid for construction work at the Mountain Distribution Center, Mountaintown, West America, in accordance with Invitation to Bid No. 16 and all attachments and amendments thereto.

Our bid price is in the amount of _____ Dollars ($_____) which price includes the cost of the Performance Bond. The undersigned agrees to complete the work in _____ calendar days from the dated notification in the Owner's Authorization to Proceed, and the certified receipt thereof.

Attached hereto is a list of subcontractors whom we propose to use for those sections of work exceeding $1,000 in contract cost.

We submit the following proposals for alternates and/or substitutions.

Our total bid price is as follows:

The undersigned agrees to execute the Construction Contract Form provided with the Invitation to Bid. The undersigned certifies that it/he is:

SELECTING [and Meshing With] YOUR CONTRACTOR (continued)

BID PACKAGE EXAMPLE

1. A Corporation incorporated in the State of _____

2. A Partnership consisting of the following partners_____

_____

3. An individual/dba whose name is

_____

The foregoing offer shall be binding upon the undersigned until _____

_____.

_____
Contractor

_____   _____
                                        Date

_____
Title

_____
Address

_____
Telephone

_____
Contractor's License No.   State

Remember: Owner to maintain separate record of contractor evaluation, recommendations, etc.

EXHIBIT A

Attached to and a part of Agreement No. 16 are contract documents referred to in Article 6 the Contract.

In general, the work consists of all site earthwork and fencing as described in the attached plans and specifications for the Dry Storage Warehouse located in Mountaintown, West America.

Drawings and specifications as set forth in Article 6 Contract Documents are enumerated and included as follows:

A. Invitation to Bid
B. Bid Form
C. General Conditions
D. Special Conditions
E. Technical Specifications
    1. Section E-1, Site Grading and Compaction
    2. Section E-2, Fencing and Gates
F. Drawings

Number	Rev. No.	Date
C1		
A1		
S1		

G. Owner-Furnished Items
H. Owner's Construction Schedule

MAKING DEAL

SELECTING [and Meshing With] YOUR CONTRACTOR [continued]

OFFICE PARK; 22,413 s.f. [3 buildings]; actual project

	BASE BID (000)	DAYS TO COMPLETE	ALT.#1 DBL. GLAZE	ALT.#2 RET. WALLS	ALT.#3 T-BAR CLG.	ALT.#4 TINTED GLASS	ALT.#5 2&8 AC
"A"	$1.213	210	$13,079	$67,422	$26,000	$8,494	$7,800
"B"	$1.350	180	$12,520	$15,215	1.61/sf	$8,135	$11,000
"C"	$1.394	300	$12,379	$15,900	$14,696	$8,294	No Bid
"D"	$1.461	210	$12,175	$30,394	1.18/sf	$7,912	$10,700
"E"	$1.646	240	$33,333	$61,836	1.45/sf	$9,928	$7,889

NOTE; "A" is only "local" bidder. Offices of others are 45-90 minutes away

Base bid DOES NOT include tenant improvements

QUESTION: What do you notice in the bid breakdowns which could lead to
cost overruns or problems in the future?

MAKING DEAL

SELECTING (and Meshing With) YOUR CONTRACTOR (continued)

BASIC ELEMENTS OF THE OWNER - CONTRACTOR AGREEMENT

NOTE: As with the Architectural Agreement, understand there is no <u>perfect</u> contract. These provisions will eliminate much of the potential problems, however.

Scope of Work
Outline clearly in the body of the contract what the work is; where it is, (including A.P.#), and what the cost is.

Cost
a. Lump sum; for small projects only
b. Cost plus Fixed Fee; with defined "schedule of values" including OH&P
c. Time and Materials (T&M); used <u>only where there are true unknowns</u>
d. Unit Prices; rarely used in building construction.......mostly for public works projects

Progress Payments
Specify when payment will be made, and special circumstances to take advantage of lumber discounts ("2%-10th prox.") and glulam products (5% if paid 10 days from date of invoice), etc. <u>Usually</u> a 10% retention is held on <u>all</u> work. However, some residential lenders will pay in full until the last draw; retaining 10% of the last draw amount until the lien period is past. This means that the landscaper, painter, paving contractor and others doing work on the final portions of the project will not be paid, even a partial payment until well after the project is completed.

Time Schedule
The work shall commence no later than_____; the work shall be completed no later than_____. Completion is defined as Final Inspection approval, and/or issuance of the Certificate of Occupancy by the____(appropriate authority)_____.

The contract shall provide schedule as part of the contract documents.
NOTE: Do Not Use "Substantial Completion" to Define Completion Date
Delays And Extension Of Time
- Define what are delays which may cause an extension
- What is the elapsed time after first observance of the condition to make a claim? 15-30 days seems reasonable. What you <u>don't want</u> is a series of claims coming through just as the project is being finished and final payments are being made

Liquidated Damages
See Appendix for additional comments; reference to Civil Code 1675 and 1676
Provision is valid unless the party seeking to invalidate the provision established that the provision was unreasonable under the circumstances existing at the time the contract was made. (Civil Code, Title 4.5, Liquidated Damages, Chapter 1, General Provisions 1671 [b]) California law <u>may</u> now favor <u>reasonable</u> liquidated provisions. Conflicting cases leave unresolved the question of whether a liquidated damages clause will be enforced against a contractor when part of the delay is caused by the contractor and part by the owner.

REMEMBER: If the liquidated damages provision is construed as a penalty, it is unenforceable under California Law
Arbitration
- Binding or non-binding?
- Specified amount of hours of mediation prior to arbitration may be valuable
- American Arbitration Association, Construction Industry Rules is commonly specified. However, there are other competent arbitration venues
- "Reasonable" (or actual) attorneys' fees awarded to prevailing party. **Also "Expert Witness" fees to prevailing party. Not <u>normally</u> included**

MAKING DEAL

SELECTING (and Meshing With) YOUR CONTRACTOR (continued)
BASIC ELEMENTS OF THE OWNER - CONTRACTOR AGREEMENT (continued)

Arbitration * (continued)
Unless otherwise agreed in writing, Contractor shall continue the work required to be performed by Contractor under the Contract, and Owner shall continue to make payments to the Contractor on all work which is not the subject of any dispute between the parties.

Final Payment And Release
- Owner files Notice of Completion within ten (10) days after date of completion (see previous for definition of "completion") with the County Recorder in the County in which the work is located. NOTE: Title Company can handle this.
- Final Payment(s) to contractor(s) 35 days after filing such notice.
- Lien releases from Contractor and Sub-Contractors; also for "Progress Payments" (see p. 70)

Changes In The Work (Change Orders and Extra Work)
- Determine time for number of days <u>"after first observance of the 'changed condition'"</u>
- Time limit to file a claim for extra work.......15 days is reasonable?
- Contractor to provide, <u>as part of bid</u>, hourly labor rates (or unit prices) for the major crafts to assist with determining fair compensation for extra work
- Disputes as to change order amounts shall not cause cessation of work
- Contractor's OH&P: <u>don't have it a fixed percentage on all work.</u> Reasonable might be 5% on work by others; 15% on work under general contractor's <u>direct</u> "care, custody and control"
- Consider lump sum in base bid for general contractor's OH&P on change orders

Owners Right To Terminate
See A.I.A. A201 - General Conditions, 1987; Article 14. Can be complicated and potentially a matter for litigation

Surveys, Permits and Regulations
- Owner to furnish base line and some elevation benchmarks
- Owner to obtain and pay for <u>all</u> building permits and appropriate development fees

Protection of Work, Property and Persons
The contractor shall adequately protect the work, adjacent property and the public, and shall be responsible for any damage or injury due to his act or neglect <u>specifically including "vandalism and malicious mischief."</u> Address scaffolding and temporary security fencing if appropriate.

Inspection of Work   ]
Correction of Work   ] - standard clauses in all construction contracts
Cleaning Up   ]

Conditions Affecting The Work
The contractor shall be responsible for having taken steps necessary to ascertain the nature and location of the work, and the general, local and subsurface conditions which can affect the work or the cost therof.

* Signing a contract having a binding arbitration clause <u>may</u> result in an arbitration award which is contrary to law and not subject to judicial review or appeal. <u>Consider</u> using a carefully drafted arbitration clause (or agreement) which establishes the arbitrator to follow the substantive law of the state.

SELECTING (and Meshing With) YOUR CONTRACTOR (continued)
BASIC ELEMENTS OF THE OWNER - CONTRACTOR AGREEMENT (continued)

Conditions Affecting The Work (continued)
Failure by the Contractor to do so will not relieve him from responsibility for successfully performing the work without additional expense to the Owner.
Add language as to no representations by Owner unless in writing; and representations by owner must be stated expressly in the contract.
This general language should be included in the bidding documents, if a formal bidding procedure is used.
Insurance
Generally Contractor's **minimum** limits of $1,000,000 and $300,000 for comprehensive public liability and property damage respectively. Liability insurance shall include all major divisions of coverage, and be on a comprehensive basis:
1. Premises/Operations (including C, V, and X coverage as applicable)
2. Independent Contractor's Protective
3. Products and Completed Operations
4. Personal Injury Liability with Employment Exclusion Deleted
5. Contractual, including specified provisions for Contractor's obligations under A.I.A. (1987) - A201 General Conditions
6. Owned, non-owned and hired motor vehicles
7. Broad Form Property Damage, including Completed Operations
8. Such insurance as will protect Contractor (and Owner) from claims under Workers' Compensation Acts
Assignment And Safety- standard clauses in construction contracts
Materials, Appliances, Employees and Superintendence
Materials and equipment shall be new and of the best quality. Contractor shall submit samples, etc. Workmen skilled in their trades. Contractor shall keep on his work, during its progress, a competent superintendent or foreman satisfactory to the Owner. See also A.I.A. (1976) 4.3.1 and 4.9.1 re: "superintendence".
Separate Contracts, Acceptance of Work By Others
If any part of the Contractor's work depends for proper execution or results upon the work of any other Contractor, this Contractor shall inspect and promptly report to the Owner any defects in such work which render it unsuitable for such proper execution and results. His failure to so inspect and report shall constitute an acceptance of the other Contractor's work as fit and proper for the reception of his work, except as to defects which may develop in the other Contractor's work after the execution of his work.
Sub-Contracts By Contractor
- Nothing contained in the Contract shall create any contractual relation between the Owner and any Sub-Contractor
- General Contractor responsible for work of Sub-Contractors
- Owner to assume warranty call-backs (not warranty itself) of Sub-Contractors? If so, include with bidding information and documents
- Contract documents part of any sub-contracts
  NOTE: Very important for arbitration clause; only signatories can participate, but non-signatories (i.e. Sub-Contractors) will participate if the subcontract incorporates the terms of the underlying Owner/General Contractor Agreement
- Provide list of Sub-Contractors and vendors

SELECTING (and Meshing With) YOUR CONTRACTOR (continued)
BASIC ELEMENTS OF THE OWNER - CONTRACTOR AGREEMENT (continued)

Sanitation
Contractor shall furnish suitable conveniences for workmen, keep them in proper condition and at the completion of the work, disinfect and remove all such facilities. Approved chemical toilets are acceptable.

Disposal
All material not to be salvaged or re-used as indicated on the drawings or in the specifications shall be disposed of off the Owner's property by the Conractor, and at the Contractor's expense. **Particularly address toxic or hazardous waste material if such is expected to exist at the site.**

Lines, Grades, Stakes and Datum
Owner shall establish a base line and one (1) bench mark in the vicinity of the work for the use of Contractor. Clearly define cost responsibility for any other reference points. Contractor shall be responsible for checking all dimensions as a whole and in detail, and shall lay out and become responsible for the exact position(s) and elevation(s) of all parts of the work. Any errors by the Contractor shall be altered, removed, or replaced at the Contractor's sole expense as the Owner may direct.

Temporary Utilities and Services
Contractor shall make his own arrangements for temporary utilities which may be required such as electrical power, water, telephone, heat, temporary office facility, security, or fencing as may be appropriate.

Protection of Existing Improvement
Define clearly the responsibility and what the "improvements" are.

Drawings
Refer again to p. 71 and 74 for Architect's ommissions.
Ommissions from the drawings or the misdescription of details of work which are manifestly necessary to carry out the intent of the drawings or which are customarily performed, shall not relieve the Contractor from performing such omitted or misdescribed details of work, and they shall be performed as if fully and correctly set forth and described in the drawings.
NOTE: This provision avoids "Gee, I didn't know you wanted doors!" as in working with outline specifications!
In case of conflict between the Base Contract and these General Conditions, the General Conditions shall govern. In case of conflict between the drawings and the specifications, the specifications shall govern.

The Contractor shall correct all drawings to show changes made during construction (especially underground utilities and tenant improvements [if applicable]) **and shall furnish the Owner with one (1) set of "as-built" reproduceable transparencies of the corrected drawings.**
NOTE: There will be lots of "squawks" about this. However, strictly enforce the provision and do not release final payment(s) until "as-builts" are received. They may be invaluable in the future. List all drawings, contract documents, soils reports, including the caveat that sub-contractors are in possessions of these. "Contractor shall familiarize himself with the Grading, Architectural, Structural, Plumbing, Mechanical,and Electrical drawings and specifications and plan his work to conform to the conditions noted so as to facilitate the combined work of all trades."

MAKING DEAL

SPECIAL REPORT NO. 7 - MANAGING CONSTRUCTION CLAIMS
How To Avoid Them; What To Do When They Are Unavoidable

FROM: Mark Noe

Construction disputes arise usually from [1] imprecise, incomplete or poorly crafted agreements, technical specifications or working drawings, [2] agreements with a bias to one of the parties and [3] failure of the contractors to perform their work in accordance with the contract documents or appropriate industry "standards of care". And occasionally, reasonable people have an honest dispute or misunderstanding which must be resolved. Occasionally.

The principal reasons for disputes are [1] failure of the project to be delivered in a timely manner or in accordance with the specified completion date and/or [2] quality of work not in conformance with the specifications or industry standards and [3] compensation/definition of "extra work".

Many feel the first cause or reason (timely delivery) is relieved, or even eliminated, by a liquidated damages clause (for commentary see my Special Report No. 3). This simply is not so. As noted in the report, if there is valid concern about on-time delivery by the low bidder, perhaps another, more reliable contractor should be retained.

Anent quality of workmanship: You should consider hiring an independent, qualified inspector or construction manager for weekly or semi-monthly inspections, in addition to the periodic inspections (supposed to be) performed by the design team. While this may be a "premium" expense, the relatively minor cost will save you major headaches in wending your way through the construction maze and avoiding costly retrofitting solutions thereafter.

Finally, a very strong recommendation: Even with proper due-diligence, attention to detail and well drafted contract documents, you still may have problems; e.g., a "change order artist" contractor slipped by the screening process, drawings which seemed complete are not, lender draws and inspections are not timely, etc. As these problems compound, there is only one thing to do: **STOP THE PROJECT**. This will not be painless; maybe alienating prospective tenants or buyers, causing interest cost hikes, possibly terminating consulting or construction agreements, or the like. However, stopping the project and resolving the problem(s) ultimately will be far less painful (and costly) than continuing "as-is". Of that you may be assured.

Additional expert commentary on the subject follows:

Lee Saylor, Saylor Consulting Group; Nationally recognized, the Saylor name is synonymous with accurate, on-time cost estimates and well prepared, thoughtful forensic investigation and testimony:

"Complex construction litigation" has evolved in the court system because construction cases usually are taken off the fast track calendar. Typically, when a plaintiff sues a contractor defendant, the contractor will bring a complaint against subcontractors and (likely) the architect and consulting engineers. The litigation may be escalated, often with twenty or more parties involved. Motions, interrogatories, discovery and depositions can continue for years. There must be a better way!

The expense of construction litigation has caused parties to rethink the process leading to new strategies, among which are "partnering" and "alternative dispute resolutions"; each show significant signs of easing the problem of construction claims. **Partnering** shows signs of altering a potentially adversarial relationship by turning them (owner, architect, contractor) into allies, building a unified team which can solve a problem by working together rather than against each other. Partnering is a concept which should be implemented at the project start; its emphasis is on claims avoidance.

MANAGING CONSTRUCTION CLAIMS (continued)

Lee Saylor, Saylor Consulting Group (continued)

With **Alternative Dispute Resolution** (aka A.D.R.), the adversarial relationship does not vanish, but may avoid the cost of protracted litigation. Construction litigation often is so complex that a judge, inexperienced in construction matters, may make the litigation move faster by appointing a "special master". The special master often is an attorney or retired judge who can convince the parties involved to find a path which resolves the dispute(s). Usually it will involve attorneys and experts for the litigating parties and a capable mediator, able to convince the parties there is room for a compromise, leading to an equitable solution. Such a compromise is almost always honed in shades of gray rather than blacks and whites.

Obviously, neither Partnering nor A.D.R. will solve all construction disputes. Owners, contractors, subcontractors, architects and engineers can benefit from both concepts, and all segments of the industry have much to gain. And as A.D.R. rarely occurs before the end of a project, Partnering would seem to be, if not the wave of the future, at least a ripple flowing against the tide of litigation.

Tom Reeves, Reeves and Associates; since 1978, Tom's firm has specialized exclusively in construction claims, claims management and litigation support. Reeves is qualified as an expert by State and Federal Courts in California, Oregon and Washington. Following are Reeves' Commandments....20, instead of 10:

1. Never pick a fight you cannot win. Sometimes it's better to walk away.
2. A bad contract is not worth doing.
3. Construction is a business and should be run as one; the goal is obvious.
4. Mistakes in the planning stage are cheap; mistakes in production are not.
5. Pick your time and place to admit a problem. Control the outcome.
6. Never fail on a claim for lack of Notice, Default or Waiver.
7. The contract includes Bidding Documents, General Conditions, Supplementary Conditions, Drawings and Addenda; in short...everything!
8. Time is money; it also is less threatening.
9. No one wants to do a bad job. Good management assures that they don't.
10. Every project has problems. The successful Contractor (or Owner) is the one who anticipates them with resolution to their benefit.
11. **If it hasn't been written, it hasn't been said.**
12. Do not mistake an adversary for a fool. They are holding something you are trying to get.
13. Why would you abuse someone you are trying to get to give you money (or other consideration)? Respect is contagious.
14. The most compelling language in the development of a claim is: Your attention and direction in this matter (problem/request/situation) is required.
15. **Don't let someone else make their problem your problem.**
16. When in doubt....read the instructions or ask.
17. The quicker a dispute is resolved, the less it costs...time, money and emotions.
18. Keep your truths simple.
19. **Truth is fact. Facts are compelling.**
20. Hang them with their own rope.

Bob Field, an attorney with Field, Richardson & Wilhelmy in Walnut Creek specializes in construction disputes, professional liability and property damage cases. He also serves as an arbitrator and mediator; and as a special master and judge in mini trials on construction and real estate cases.
PRE-PLANNING PROGRAM Owners and developers seeking to avoid construction claims must commit early to a no-claims strategy and carry it through the whole construction process.
DESIGN Select an architect or engineer who has a record of producing good construction documents. Working documents for the improvement should be complete and accurate. The owner, and ultimately the architect or engineer, impliedly warrants the plans and specifications to be complete, accurate and workable. Allocate sufficient funds and time for the design so as to produce good working drawings. Errors, omissions and ambiguities plant the seeds which later bloom into costly and time consuming construction claims.

MANAGING CONSTRUCTION CLAIMS (continued)

Bob Field; Field, Baker & Richardson (continued)

PRE-CONSTRUCTION   Screen contractors very carefully in a pre-qualification process. Consider bids only from contractors with track records for completing projects on time and within budget. Remember, the lowest bid is not always the best bid, and may result in a higher cost of construction. Hold pre-bid and pre-construction conferences with contractors so as to open the lines of communication, answer questions and clarify ambiguities as soon as possible. Use a well-drafted construction contract which has clearly defined procedures for timely notice and documentation of any claim.

CONSTRUCTION   Develop a good working relationship among the owner, contractor and architect, based upon familiarity with and fair application of the contract documents. Have weekly construction meetings on site and issue minutes of the meetings to all appropriate and interested parties. Promptly resolve issues and potential disputes early and document them. Require updated work schedules. Have a clearly defined procedure for authorizing extra work and change orders, and follow that procedure. Act promptly and decisively on requests for extra compensation or time extensions, based upon the documented facts. With each progress payment, obtain lien waivers and releases from the contractor and his subcontractors and suppliers. If there are disputes during construction, attempt to have them resolved by negotiation as soon as possible.

COMPLETION   Hold additional meetings at the time of substantial completion and final punch list completion. See that all open issues or latent disputes have been resolved or defined clearly as to scope and claim. Obtain from the contractor a signed receipt and release of claims on final payments. If there is a claim, have it clearly defined as an exception to the release. Obtain unconditional lien waivers and releases on final payment from the contractor, subcontractors and suppliers.

CONCLUSION   If the owner/developer insists on good design documents, a proper contract, defined procedures and notice provision, hands-on contract administration and fair and open communication among the design team with good documentation, the quantity and dollar amount of claims will be eliminated or restricted greatly.

Sean Absher, Attorney-at-Law; Miller, Starr & Regalia; Mr. Absher, a shareholder of the firm, has broad litigation practice including construction claims, easement and property disputes and varying liability matters pertaining to real estate:

Sometimes a developer, owner, contractor or subcontractor is involved in a construction dispute which does not lend itself to prompt and efficient resolution. Informal attempts at resolving the dispute are unsuccessful. Indeed, if anything, the dispute can take a more strident posture as further meetings only aggravate and crystallize the parties' position(s). It now appears that the dispute is headed toward the high cost and uncertainty of state court litigation. Statistically, there is a 95% chance that the case will settle before trial, but not before the parties have spent tens of thousands of dollars (perhaps hundreds) in attorneys' fees, court costs and expert and consultant fees. This scenario, which is all too common, need not happen. With some foresight, the parties effectively can eliminate the possibility of state court litigation while ensuring that their dispute is resolved in a cost efficient manner by an unbiased and competent third party. One well known method is binding arbitration.

Under California statutory law, an arbitration provision is enforceable only against signatories to the contract containing an arbitration provision. Generally, non-signatories must consent to being made parties to the arbitration. However, a signatory should not overlook the fact that non-signatories whose contract incorporates documents which contain an arbitration provision may be subject to the incorporated arbitration provision, a scenario usually arising where the subcontract incorporates the terms of the underlying owner/general contractor agreement, which does contain an arbitration provision.

A "good" arbitration provision should have the following terms:

1.   Clear definition of the nature of the dispute subject to submission to arbitration (e.g., "all disputes arising from the contract or related to performance or interpretation of the contract").
2.   Clear statement in the clause that the arbitration is binding and final.
3.   An award of reasonable attorneys' fees, court costs, expert witness fees, arbitration cost and arbitrator's compensation to the prevailing party.
4.   Method for selecting arbitrator and rules and procedures governing arbitration (e.g., clause stating that arbitration and selection of the arbitrator are governed by American Arbitration Association, Construction Industry Rules).

MANAGING CONSTRUCTION CLAIMS (continued)

Sean Absher; Miller, Starr & Regalia (continued)

5. Incorporation of the civil discovery statute in construction projects likely to require civil discovery in the event of a dispute.
6. Manner in which arbitration fees and arbitrator's costs are to be paid if different from tribunal's general rules.

MN Note: It is very interesting to observe that all commentary was prepared sans a predetermined topical format and scope. And while each contributor had a slightly different "spin" on the topic, each arrived at basically the same end result and conclusions. Interesting.

The foregoing subject matter is intended as general information only, and is not intended as legal advice. Persons with specific legal matters should consult competent and appropriate counsel concerning anything which may affect their particular legal positions.

For additional dialogue on this topic or other real estate, development or construction matters, please contact:

Mark W. Noe
Sloane Development
770 Third Street East
Sonoma, CA 95476
(925) 939-8707 or (707) 938-2738

Leland S. Saylor
Saylor Consulting Group
12 Geary St., 7th Floor
San Francisco, CA 94108
(415) 291-3200

Thomas P. Reeves
Reeves & Associates
354-27th Street
San Francisco, CA 94131
(415) 641-9798

Robert C. Field
Field, Richardson & Wilhelmy
2033 No. Main Street #900
Walnut Creek, CA 94596
(925) 934-7700

Sean B. Absher
Miller, Starr & Regalia
1331 No. California Blvd., 5th Floor
Walnut Creek, CA 94596
(925) 935-9400

KEY ELEMENTS IN THE LEASE

TYPES OF LEASES

DEAL POINTS

Premises	Occupancy Type
Use	Commencement Date
Term	Rent/Increases/Deposits
Options	

IMPORTANT BOILERPLATE

Possession	Pass Thrus (reimbuseables)
Maintenance	Assignment and Subletting
Alterations	Default
Insurance	Late Fees
Addenda and Exhibits	

MAKING DEAL

LEASE INGREDIENTS

Standard Industrial [or Commercial] Lease; American Industrial Real Estate Association [or equivalents]. **Don't use "Landlord's Lease" or Stationary Store Lease!**

Delay In Commencement [a] when is "drop dead" date for delivery of premises,and [b] can tenant have early access for fixturization.

Rent/Security Deposit [a] money paid upon execution of the lease, [b] last month's rent [without interest?] as security, and [c] free rent, if any.

Maintenance, Repairs, And Alterations If net-net-net, then "Repairs of inherent structural defects shall be by Lessor"; otherwise define what charges Lessee pays as painting, roofing, paving, etc.

Insurance Indemnity [a] liability insurance - $1,000,000 **minimum**, [b] property insurance — valuation? how updated?, [c] Waiver of Subrogation: Lessee and lessor hereby waive right of recovery against each other. Insuring party required to give notice to the insurance carrier that the mutual waiver of subrogation is contained in the lease.

Insurer's right of subrogation: If loss is caused by someone else's negligence, the insurer has the right to sue the negligent 3rd party for the amount it paid the insured under their policy.

Damage Or Destruction Partial [insured/un-insured], total destruction, and damage near the end of the term. Can be major problem; rebuild?

Personal And Real Property Taxes segregation thereof

Broker's Fees when, how, and to whom paid; list fee amount?

Insuring Party who is responsible for <u>obtaining</u> [not paying for] the insurance?

Rent Adjustment when? subject to Consumer Price Index [CPI]? cumulative or not? which index?

Property Tax Increases re-assessment as a result of a sale

Arbitration condition precedent to litigation? which arbitration association? binding?

Lease Guarantee have competent review of this. Can be tricky.

Execution Of Lease who executes? by corporation <u>and</u> individuals if closely held company, proper execution if a corporation.

Option To Extend/Purchase <u>always</u> have a separate agreement if for a purchase option....do not include in lease

Life Insurance on key person/personnel of Lessee?

Financial Information net worth, credit rating report, bank reference, etc.

Hazardous Materials Lessee's responsibility thereof

Code Upgrades responsibility for; i.e. earthquake, HDCP, etc.

MAKING DEAL

LEASE INGREDIENTS [continued]

Factors to Determine "Fair Market Value" in Rental Renewal Options
Quality, age, and condition of the building, especially if formal valuation procedures
Leased "as-is" without additional expense
Rent abatements which may be then existing
Takeover or assumption costs for new tenant

Chronic Defaults; Cured in Applicable Periods
Default of any obligation more than 3 times in the past 12 months: such default shall constitute separate
default under the lease, which default cannot be cured

Options or [Preferential] Right of First Offer
Specific time and notice prodecure for optionee to accept or reject; say 7-10 calendar days

Toxic Liability Caused by Others
Consult with competent counsel for laws, rules, and requirements.

Right to Sublet
Consult with a very good real estate attorney! The law, seemingly, is becoming muddy. Share in any
sublet profits?

Tenant Default After Rent Concessions [free rent]
Stagger periods of free rent; not all at front
Tenant still pays full pass-through expenses
Any default: owes all of the base rent [whether used or not?]. Default is for any lease condition

Tax Escalation Clauses
Improvements [by tenant] to tenant's own space may be the responsibility of lessor. Specify taxes
"attributable to improvements"

Enforcement of Use Clause [probable retail use]
eg. "All window displays must be maintained and operated in a first-class manner, similar to standards set
by [say] Nordstrom", i.e., name a well-known local store and require the tenant to follow its standards.
Be precise as to standards

Percentage Rents
How about [common] practice of 10% "no-rings" (on cash register)? applies mainly to retail.
"Slotting allowances" [new products on shelves] and other promotional fees
Gross sales include: "All amounts received by tenant from conducting business
on or from the leased space"

NOTE: Leasing law appears to be undergoing rapid evolution. Periodically review
      boilerplate lease language

Shopping Center World
6151 Powers Ferry Road N.W.
Atlanta, GA 30339–2941
(770) 955–2500

LEASE LANGUAGE

Proposals Demand Careful Attention

Although letters of intent can be helpful tools in nailing down major points, they also can become sources of liability.

By Steven B. Arbuss

Lease negotiations often begin with the preparation of a document that outlines the basic terms and conditions for the proposed lease. This document, also known as a lease proposal, letter of intent or memorandum of business terms, is usually intended to be a non-binding statement of the major deal points. A typical lease prosposal might contain a description of the premises and the rent, and an estimate of the extra charges the tenant will have to pay. Proposals also are used to establish the basic terms for lease terminations, modifications and assignments. Although this sort of document can be useful — by setting negotiation guidelines and confirming the parties' interest in the deal, for example — there is always a risk that a lease proposal may give rise to liability.

Courts in a number of jurisdictions have interpreted letters of intent as binding agreements, on the basis that the parties have agreed to definite terms and intend to be bound. Indeed, a lease may be found to exist despite specific language in the proposal that it is intended to be non-binding or that the business terms are subject to a board of directors' approval. Even if the document itself is not interpreted as an enforceable contract, a court might find an implied agreement or duty on the part of the parties to continue lease negotiations in good faith.

While there is no guaranteed so-lution to the legal risks created by letters of intent, there are a few general guidelines. The lease proposal:

• should contain language stating that the parties do not intend to be bound by the document and that no contract will exist until a formal lease is executed and delivered by both parties.

• should state that significant terms and conditions of the lease remain to be negotiated, and should give examples where possible.

• might expressly negate any obligation of the parties to continue negotiations.

• should state that it does not constitute a reservation of space or an option to lease the premises.

It may be helpful to set out some or all of these provisions prominently in the document, perhaps in bold print, and, if there is particular concern, to have each party initial the provisions. Language similar to the foregoing provisions also should be included in any draft leases submitted for review.

The conduct of the parties also is important. For example, congratulatory statements between leasing representatives, or subsequent communications acknowledging that there is "a deal" between the landlord and tenant or that the parties have "a lease" could be interpreted as intent to be bound by the lease proposal. While landlords like to encourage tenants to prepare for construction and opening while the lease is still under negotiation, some acts — such as preparation and approval of plans, commencement of tenant improvement work, or occupancy and payment of rent by the tenant — could be viewed as partial performance creating a binding agreement.

Care should be taken regarding the accuracy of any information set forth in the lease proposal. When describing the tenant's obligations to contribute to taxes and common area maintenance, for example, a statement might be included that the specified charges are current estimates that are subject to change and/or adjustment under the lease. It also may be advisable to state that the listing of monetary charges under the proposal is not be be construed as an exhaustive list of all amounts that will be payable under the lease.

In all cases, the form of lease proposal should be reviewed by an attorney familiar with the jurisdiction in which the center is located.

The use of lease proposals is an established procedure for many developers and national tenants, and, in most cases, there is probably no reason to abandon the process. However, leasing representatives should always keep in mind the possibility that, if care is not taken, a lease proposal might be construed as a binding agreement. □

Steven B. Arbuss is a partner in the law firm of Pircher, Nichols & Meeks, Los Angeles.

Shopping Center World
6151 Powers Ferry Road N.W.
Atlanta, GA 30339-2941
(770) 955-2500

LEASE LANGUAGE

Appraising Rent Escalations

By Sheldon A. Halpern

The lack of attention given to lease language dealing with fair rental value escalations is surprising. Complex language and careful contingency planning are often associated with lease provisions dealing with occurrences like casualty and condemnation. In contrast, fair rental value escalations often are described in brief, conceptual language.

Because fair rental value escalations are used in various contexts (i.e., options to renew, options to expand and periodic rental increases) and in various types of leases (i.e., space leases, leases of entire buildings and ground leases), it is important that the issues described below are considered in the context of each situation, with the lease tailored accordingly.

• **Method for determining.** The most generally accepted method for determining fair rental value is an appraisal. The parties should be given a specific time period to agree upon the rent and then, failing that, a specific time period to agree upon a single appraiser. Failing agreement upon a single appraiser, the appraisal can be conducted by three appraisers — one appointed by each party and the third appointed by the first two appraisers. All appraisers should be members of a generally recognized professional appraisal organization and should have significant experience in appraising the specific type of property under consideration. The lease should specify whether the rent determined by the appraiser(s) can be less than the rent payable prior to the escalation period.

• **Time for determining.** This issue is of particular significance if the fair rental value escalation is related to the exercise of an option. The landlord will seek to have the appraisal conducted near the end of the existing term (on the assumption that rents tend to rise), and the tenant will seek to have the appraisal conducted before it is required to exercise its option (so it will know the rent it will be paying in advance of its decision). A compromise for a major tenant might involve an appraisal after the required option exercise and a right of rescission by the tenant. The timing of the exercise of the right of rescission is important because the landlord will need time to find a replacement tenant.

• **Comparables.** The parties should consider whether to specify (or rely on the appraiser to specify at the relevant time) the land area and the type of center to be included within the scope of the

Sheldon A. Halpern is a partner in the Los Angeles-based law firm of Pircher, Nichols & Meeks.

appraisal. The landlord should seek to exclude the use of renewal leases (unless the renewal rents also were determined by reference to fair rental value), subleases and leases with tenants that have an equity interest in the center.

• **Use assumptions.** Appraisers should be instructed as to (1) whether to assume the highest and best use, retail use or the specific use to which the premises are being put, and (2) whether to take into account use restrictions set forth in the lease or in other documents (like reciprocal easement agreements) to which the lease is subject.

• **Assumptions as to improvements.** Particularly in connection with ground leases, the parties should make sure the appraisers understand whether to appraise the property as vacant land or as then improved, and whether to consider the physical characteristics of the site (including soil and waste problems and accessibility of utilities) and applicable zoning and other governmental approval restrictions.

• **Concessions.** Appraisers should be given guidance as to how to deal with concessions like tenant improvement allowances and rent-free periods. They may not be applicable (or may be only partially applicable) to those fair rental escalation situations in which it is unlikely that the tenant will need to remodel its premises. The lease should specify whether the rent otherwise payable will be reduced if no brokerage commission is payable by the landlord in context of the event triggering the fair rental value escalation.

• **Additional and percentage rent.** These should specify how the parties intend to deal with common area maintenance (CAM) costs after the fair rental value escalation. For example, if the existing lease utilizes a base year approach, the appraiser should be advised as to whether to assume that CAM costs will be handled in the manner in which they are then typically handled in the relevant leasing market (as distinguished from merely retaining the same base year or moving to a current base year). The appraiser also should be advised as to whether to adjust its determination of fair rental value to take into account the amount of percentage rent being paid by the tenant.

Failure to deal specifically with the issues outlined above could result in confusion and disputes as to the aspect of a lease that is most important to both parties — the rent.

MAKING DEAL

CONSTRUCTION MANAGEMENT AND COST CONTROL
Bruce Moen, PE

INTRODUCTION
Agreements for Construction Management (CM) should include elements reviewed previously for other consultants and contractors

CONSTRUCTION MANAGEMENT
Types: General Contractor, Broker-Builder and from the '70s the professional CM, defined as: part of a 3-party team (contractor, architect, owner); non-adversarial; provides construction leadership and coordination as the owner's representative. Provides alternatives for schedules, cost impacts (aka value engineering), and advises on material lead time, work packaging and local practices. In the truest sense, the CM does not perform construction work with its own forces.

CLIENT OBJECTIVES FOR THE PROJECT (all in sync)
Cost - within budget
Time - completed within the agreed upon time frame
Performance - of value and quality

ORGANIZATION AND CONTRACT ALTERNATIVES
Jobsite Organization and Setup
Management Methods and Contract Choice - fixed price, cost + fee or guaranteed
  maximum price
Traditional - designer, general contractor, sub-contractors, owner
Turnkey
Professional Construction Management - all as a team

SCHEDULE ALTERNATIVES
Traditional - all drawings completed, bid out, bar or critical path schedule
Phased Approach - aka "fast track". Requires knowledge and experience

WHY USE CONSTRUCTION MANAGEMENT? - ADVANTAGES TO OWNER
Specialized construction skills; no conflict of interest
Independent and continuing evaluation of project
Coordination of design and construction
Price competition maintained
Long or short term savings with Value Engineering

RESPONSIBILITIES OF A CONSTRUCTION MANAGER
To Owner - keep fully informed; work within delegation; sound advice
To Designer - professional cooperation; mutual project goals
To Contractor(s) - administration; interpret plans/specs; inspections

CONSTRUCTION MANAGEMENT AND COST CONTROL (continued)

DUTIES - SUMMARY
Construction Manager - planning, pre-qualification of contractors and their sub-contractors, reasonable cost estimates, supervision/coordination, contract administration, Owner - funding the project, A&E contract(s), prompt decisions, prompt payments to all parties

SELECTING A CONSTRUCTION MANAGER
Prequalification- references, resume, scope and size of prior work
Compensation and Fees - hourly or monthly rate; rare if a lump sum due to project timing,
     Never pay as a percentage of cost
Jobsite setup and administration
Contract forms to be used
Clearly defined scope of duties

Excerpt from an article by John L. Tishman, Chairman and CEO, Tishman Realty & Construction Co., Inc. which appeared in Buildings Magazine (no longer in business), July, 1989:

The heart of the construction management concept is that the construction manager should, at all times, operate as the owner's agent and manager of all facets of the building process. The construction manager should arrange for the selection of all required specialists, seeing to it that their efforts are coordinated from the start of the design process and right on to completion and occupancy. This approach, requiring the combined efforts of the owner, construction manager, and architect is a true team approach. Through it, the owner and architect have the necessary resources to analyze design and system alternatives and their impact on cost and schedule. The most important aspect here is that the owner is made totally aware of aesthetic, schedule and cost tradeoffs before making program and design decisions.

With the construction manager acting in his overall management capacity, each segment of construction is contracted separately between the individual trade contractors and the CM, serving as the owner's agent. It should be clear that a major benefit of the CM approach is that any given trade contractor can be replaced without affecting the whole job.

NOTE: This commentary from a very large and sophisticated owner/developer differs slightly from Bruce Moen's commentary. However, as was discussed in the Contracting/Construction section, this process is, by far, the most economical and efficient manner in which to proceed. Owner/developers of substantial substance and experience often have their own construction managers on their payroll.

MAKING DEAL

THE ROLE OF PROPERTY MANAGEMENT IN DEVELOPMENT
Deborah Rothstein, CPM

I. DEFINE PROPERTY MANAGEMENT
A. Areas of Responsibility

II. PHASES OF THE DEVELOPMENT PROCESS
A. **Conceptual Stage**
   1. Existing vs. New buildings
   2. Site
   3. Target Market
   4. Financial Proforma
B. **Planning Stage**
   1. Marketing/Marketability Study
   2. Design
   3. Marketing Plan
C. **Construction Stage**
   1. Inspections
   2. Public Relations
D. **Operational Stage**
   1. Tenant Services
   2. Operations - daily and long term
   3. Financial Analysis and Reporting

III. OBJECTIVE OF PROPERTY MANAGEMENT
A. Increase Revenue
B. Improve Cash Flow
C. Increase Revenue-Producing Occupancy
D. Improve Quality of Service to Tenants
E. Improve Facilities Management
F. Tighten Cash Management Controls
G. Prepare Accurate and Timely Financial Management Reports
H. Documents for Litigation [if needed to "relocate" tenant]

ASSET MANAGEMENT The efficient use of capital, market knowledge, and planning to strengthen [...the product's...] financial position and its overall value. [Shopping Center World; Sept. '90] NOTE: What "property management" should have been doing all along?

Source Reference: **Black's Office Leasing Guide [Bay Area]**
                           760 Market St. Suite 550
                           San Francisco, CA 94102
                           [800] 300-6100

DO NOT TAKE PROPERTY MANAGEMENT FOR GRANTED! It is a craft and skill, science and art which involves substantially more than replacing toilet paper and scheduling the shampooing of carpets. 6 months of poor property management may take 12 to 18 months of great effort to get back on track. The marketplace has a very long memory and is unforgiving.

MAKING DEAL

THE ROLE OF PROPERTY MANAGEMENT IN DEVELOPMENT [continued]

Different types of properties and markets require different kinds of management at different times in the real estate cycle. Select a property manager who specializes in [and has been successful with] your type of property. The selection process proceeds identical to the other professionals on the "team" - i.e. the architect. And know the on-site manager who will be handling your project, looking through the management company, no matter how good their record and reputation.

Following are edited excerpts from "How to Profit on the Real Estate Roller Coaster" by Marvin T. Levin regarding his thoughts on Property Management:

On hiring a manager to fit your needs....for example, apartments in San Francisco are "hot", but maintenance and upkeep are key elements as much of the activity is in older buildings. This product clearly calls for managers with savvy in maintenance, not so much in marketing. Conversely, Houston's office market, which has very high vacancies (early '90s), is mostly new, Class "A" structures. Marketing skills are more important than maintenance skills here.

Property managers must do the following:
1. Market the Space. Bring potential customers to the door
2. Sell. Get people to sign and part with their money
3. Maintain the physical condition of the property
4. Provide administrative and fiscal controls

Management/marketing of property essentially consists of a series of well executed strategies to build traffic and increase the number of people who come to view your property whether for sale or lease.

Sales ability is not necessarily the same as marketing ability.

MAKING DEAL

CEL & Associates, Inc.

STRATEGIC ADVANTAGE
Fall, 1994
Issue No. K609

CEL & ASSOCIATES
12121 Wilshire Blvd.
Suite 505
Los Angeles, CA 90025

EVALUATING THE PERFORMANCE OF PROPERTY MANAGERS

Do you really know how to measure and evaluate the performance of a property manager? Is your organization stuck on the rapidly declining "manage to budget" form of performance appraisal? Do you as a property owner or as the executive with a property management operation know how the tenants feel, what their renewal intention is, and how they rate the performance of the property manager?

If you are like most real estate organizations, you probably answered the questions above with either an "I don't know" or "I think so" response. Today. competition for tenants is at the highest level in more than 20 years. Profit margins on third party management contracts are declining. and the institutionalization of ownership is requiring more accountability. To keep pace with the industry leaders. owners of real estate and those vested with directing a property management operation are measuring the performance of each property manager.

The three most important contributions management can give to staff are: (1) objective feedback on performance: (2) coaching to improve capabilities and con-

---

THE BEST TIME TO USE REACT

- To measure tenant satisfaction.
- During performance evaluations.
- When establishing annual Performance Goals.
- When taking on a new third party management contract and a Condition of the Property Report is important to convey.
- When marketing the quality of one's property management services to potential building owners.
- Throughout various leasing initiatives in which the results of a tenant satisfaction survey could make a difference.
- When setting performance improvement priorities.
- When deciding how to allocate resources to achieve the maximum benefit.
- For demonstrating the organization's commitment to quality and performance improvement.
- For comparing an entity or organization's performance to the best in the industry.
- When objectivity. independence and accuracy count.

---

tribution to client and company profitability: and (3) benchmarks to monitor and motivate future performance. While accounting statistics give one picture. they do not reveal those components of property management which are critical to long-term success such as tenant/client relations. responsiveness. follow-through. common sense and professionalism. Today's successful property management must expand and extend its evaluation techniques to be competitive.

The tool that is being used. **REACT**. was developed by CEL & Associates. Inc. in conjunction with tenants. real estate professionals. property managers. performance measurement specialists. statisticians. and business advisors. **REACT** is an independent/objective. self-administered performance measurement tool that quantifies and compares the perceptions and opinions of tenants. building owners and property managers to each other and to the scores from the best in the industry.

Utilizing the eight Business Success Factors. identified by industry experts as the benchmarks of an outstanding property management operation. the **REACT** performance measurement questionnaire: (1) identifies those performance areas in need of improvement: (2) establishes benchmarks for future performance evalu-

ations: (3) allows the users to compare their performance to the industry's best. between property managers. regions and portfolios: and (4) identifies potential renewal problems before they become unresolvable.

Creating excellence. mastering the future. and becoming a more tenant/building owner focused company requires a commitment to service and quality. By utilizing the baseline information and feedback provided by the **REACT** performance measurement program. meaningful change can and will occur. "Listen to your tenants" is becoming the mantra for the nation's leading property management companies. A desire and a goal to become a more customer-based organization is not enough. Today those who take immediate and proactive actions to evaluate and improve their performance are generally those organizations who are increasing their competitive advantage. ∎

CHARACTERISTICS OF A SUCCESSFUL CEO

- Develops a compelling vision of the firm's future.
- Translates the vision into reality by concentrating on the keys to success.
- Remains deeply involved at the very heart of things, spurring the actions necessary to carry out the vision.
- Motivates employees to embrace the vision.
- Constantly articulates the vision so that it permeates all organizational levels and functions, taking the organization where it's never been before.

Source: *Creating Excellence* by Craig Hickman and Michael Silva.

FOR MORE DETAILS

For more information and a complete package on the **REACT** Program, call (310) 571-3113 or fax your request to (310) 571-3117.

MAKING DEAL

TRUE/FALSE EXAM

T F   1. The design team [architect, engineer, etc.] should be selected
         ASAP, even before a site has been selected

T F   2. It is important for the design team to know how much experience
         you, as a developer, have in the total process

T F   3. You should always be on the lookout for other consultants even
         after you have established a good working relationship with one

T F   4. In selecting consultants, it is important to contact designers
         of buildings which you like or owners of similar facilities

T F   5. In the selection process [of consultants], you should interview
         as many firms as possible.....perhaps 6 or 8

T F   6. Compatibility of work styles is a critical element in selecting
         consultants

T F   7. If you have retained a large and prominent A&E firm, any project
         manager assigned to your project will be acceptable

T F   8. You do not need to identify the services [design, graphics, construction
         bidding/inspection, permit processing, leasing brochure,
         etc.] needed from consultants until you are pretty far along with
         the building design

T F   9. The best method for you to pay architects/engineers is a fee based
         upon the percentage of construction cost

T F   10. In the construction phase, if a job starts "sour", it is likely to
         stay that way through the duration of the project unless work is
         stopped

T F   11. It is critical to develop an "us-us" [not "us-them"] relationship/process
         with your contractor

T F   12. Your contractor should not provide "approximate" change order
         costs until precise drawings are completed

T F   13. If friends or relatives are contractors, use them as much as possible.
         Their prices will be attractive, usually

T F   14. The best bid is usually the lowest bid

T F   15. A consideration in selecting a contractor is that your project is
         no more than 25% of the contractor's volume in the preceding year

T F   16. Being your own general contractor[awarding separate sub-contracts]
         will be the least expensive, most efficient method providing you
         have time and sufficient experience to supervise the project

T F   17. Time and material contracts are the most equitable for the owner/developer

T F   18. Change order labor rates for the principal sub-contractors should
         always be included in your contract[s]

T F   19. It is not necessary to begin negotiations or bidding with a contractor
         until the working drawings are completed

T F   20. You as owner/developer need not concern yourself with the general
         or technical specifications. That will be the province of the architect or
         engineer

TRUE/FALSE EXAM (continued)

T F 21. "Design and build" performance specification contracts may be very
         attractive, particularly for electrical or HVAC work
T F 22. Deferred maintenance or value engineering are relatively unimportant
         concerns if you are doing a project solely for resale
T F 23. You should obtain as many bids as possible and, perhaps, capitalize
         on any mistakes in the bids
T F 24. Never use uninsured contractors or consultants
T F 25. "Should the contractor have known" will be a major issue in many
         change order or extra work claims
T F 26. Architects/engineers probably have errors and omissions insurance.
         They should pay for discrepancies in the drawings which cause
         change orders for extra work
T F 27. Prompt warranty call-backs and completion of the "punch list" can
         be a major problem with your contractor[s] or buyers/users
T F 28. The A.I.A. standard form construction contract is an excellent
         document to use
T F 29. [Financial] Penalties for construction delays, deducted from the
         contractor's fee, are enforceable in California
T F 30. Contract provisions should always include binding arbitration,
         thereby avoiding [possible] future litigation
T F 31. You need not double check quantity takeoffs by the architect,
         engineer, or contractor[s]. It would only be a duplication of
         efforts and wasted time
T F 32. Preliminary, yet detailed, construction cost bidding may be done
         from a single sheet showing only the site plan plus outline specifications
T F 33. The definition of "completion" is an important element in a construction
         contract
T F 34. As fair and equitable compensation for OH&P, the general contractor
         should be paid a minimum of 10% of the change order direct cost
T F 35. In determining the structural integrity of an existing building
         for re-hab, the analysis is relatively simple
T F 36. In analyzing the potential of a re-hab project, the process usually
         begins with what use may be viable
T F 37. Financing re-hab projects is usually easier because the lender can
         visualize the project better, something being already built
T F 38. Some elements of re-hab projects may lend themselves best to time
         and material contracts
T F 39. To reduce printing costs, sub-contractors need receive only those
         drawings which pertain to their portions of the work
T F 40. It is the general contractor's responsibility to file the Notice
         of Completion

APPENDIX "A"

APPRAISAL
Paul N. Farthing

I. FAIR MARKET VALUE

The most probable price, as of a specified date, in cash, or in terms equivalent to cash, or in other precisely revealed terms, for which the specified property rights should sell after reasonable exposure in a competitive market under all conditions requisite to fair sale, with the buyer and seller each acting prudently, knowledgeably, and for self interest, and assuming that neither is under duress [Whew!]

II. HIGHEST AND BEST USE

The use, from among reasonable, probable, and legal alternative uses, found to be physically possible, appropriately supported, financially feasible, and that results in the highest present land value

NOTE: No mention of market research or marketability

III. THREE APPROACHES TO VALUE

1. COST
   a. Based upon principle of substitution
   b. Generally sets upper limit value [Ed. Note: May set...]
   c. Process
   > Estimate Land Value
   > Estimate Cost of Improvements [new]
   > Estimated Accumulated Depreciation [Ed. Note: Generally
   > less significant in non-Rustbelt states]
   d. Improvement Cost less Depreciation plus Land

2. MARKET
   a. Best Indicator of Value [Ed. Note: If not in great disparity with Income Approach]
   b. Assumes a Perfect Market

3. INCOME
   a. Basic Formula

   $$\text{Value} = \frac{\text{Net Operating Income}}{\text{Cap Rate}}$$

   b. Capitalization Rate
      i. An attempt to quantify expected future benefits
      ii. Reflects the relationship between projected net income and the corresponding value thereof
      iii. The synthesis of return on investment; risk/reward expectations

   [Ed. Note: Value, as determined by income, cannot stray away for long from a (relatively) close proximity to the cost of replacement; witness Silicon Valley in the late '70s and thereafter for a while]

Ed. Note: The foregoing class outline was presented in the '80s. Subsequent difficulties with financial markets and expanded construction defects litigation require what the author calls "Valuation.....Beyond Appraisal", mandating rather sophisticated techniques of market research and computations for diminution of value and stigma and/or taint, none of which are mentioned above. Not criticism, merely commentary on changing times. A definition of stigma is provided by Chip Miles; Miles, Brummitt & Passalacqua in Walnut Creek: "Diminution in value attributable to the market's perceived risk of recurrence wher property has been repaired or stabilized; thus contemplates [a] defect - break - damage, [b] repair and [c] risk of further break".

ASBESTOS AND LEAD

Asbestos Surveys

The intent of an asbestos survey is to provide accurate information regarding location, condition, friability and asbestos content of suspect materials. All inspections are performed by EPA/OSHA certified personnel who are specifically trained to inspect and sample materials which commonly contain asbestos. Penn Environmental issues a report which enables the client to easily read and quickly reference all vital information.

Asbestos Abatement Design and Management

Penn Environmental's asbestos professionals are experienced in managing all types of asbestos projects. Trained and certified by the EPA and OSHA, Penn Environmental's building inspectors and management planners utilize the initial asbestos survey and other available information to develop an abatement design and specification. Personnel are trained in state-of-the-art, cost-effective abatement strategies and techniques. Consultants and technicians certified by Cal/OSHA perform project management activities including oversight, air monitoring and inspections.

Penn Environmental offers a variety of air monitoring services for projects of all sizes. Site surveillance technicians are certified by Cal/OSHA to perform background, personal and final air clearance sampling. Samples may be analyzed on-site by NIOSH 582 certified personnel, or at an independent AIHA laboratory. Air monitoring results are evaluated by Penn Environmental personnel and reported to the client daily.

Asbestos Operations and Maintenance Program

It is not always necessary or cost effective to remove asbestos. If asbestos is not removed, it may be necessary to develop an Operation and Maintenance (O&M) Program to monitor the condition of the asbestos containing materials and make any necessary repairs. Penn Environmental will develop and implement an O&M Program through the following:

(1) Conduct a two to four hour asbestos awareness class for maintenance and engineering personnel on the nature, uses, surveillance techniques and record keeping requirements necessary to recognize and respond to the hazards of asbestos.

(2) Notify all tenants and occupants where asbestos is present and what the potential hazards may be.

(3) Instruct tenants and occupants on how to evaluate the condition of asbestos containing materials and what should be done about them.

(4) Establish a surveillance program to monitor worker and tenant exposure to hazardous materials.

Lead Surveys/Inspections

Increasing numbers of lead inspections are requested by lenders, contractors, and governmental agencies. Lead surveys and inspections are conducted in order to determine the lead content of painted surfaces within a building. Various methods for detecting lead in paint may be utilized. Penn Environmental most frequently uses Spectrum Analyzer X-Ray Fluorescence (XRF) sampling and Atomic Absorption (AA) analysis. The AA method is often used in conjunction with the XRF machine to confirm readings. The inspection report includes a floor plan diagram of the project site to aid the client in identifying rooms and surfaces which contain lead.

Risk Assessment/Screening Risk Assessment

Building owners who are concerned with the presence of lead-based paint hazards within a structure may request an assessment of the risk posed by the lead-based paint. A risk assessment identifies the existence, nature, severity, source and location of lead-based paint and the associated exposure hazards.

While conducting a risk assessment, the risk assessor samples potential sources of lead dust such as dust within a house or in soil. If necessary, water sampling may be performed. The condition of painted surfaces is assessed, and paint chip sampling or XRF testing is performed. Recommendations on how to best manage lead-based paint to eliminate exposure hazards are provided to the client.

Workplace Consulting Services

Amid growing concerns of worker exposure to lead, especially in the construction industry, the California and Federal Departments of Occupational Safety and Health have developed regulations to reduce employee exposure. Penn Environmental provides a wide range of services for employers seeking compliance with these regulations. Services include:

- *Blood Testing*
- *Area and Personal Air Monitoring*
- *Exposure Assessments*
- *Development of an OSHA Written Compliance Plan*
- *Worker Training and Monitoring*
- *Assistance in developing safe work practices when involved in lead-related work*

Lead Abatement Design & Management

Penn Environmental's personnel are specifically trained to organize, design and manage the abatement of lead products.

Throughout a project, site technicians certified in Lead-Based Paint inspection, assessment, supervision and monitoring, sample for airborne lead concentrations both inside and outside the work area. Personal air monitoring is necessary to determine respiratory protection parameters and for employee exposure records. Upon completion of a project, additional air and surface dust monitoring is performed to assess compliance with HUD clearance guidelines.

ENVIRONMENTAL SITE ASSESSMENTS

Phase I

The initial stage of an Environmental Site Assessment is commonly referred to as a Phase 1 site assessment and is an historical review of the site. Typical tasks associated with an historical review are a "site walk-through" or inspection to identify potential contamination, regulatory agency file review, review of prior uses of the site, review of topographical maps, historical aerial photographs, geologic information and hydrologic date, and interviews with knowledgeable parties regarding the history of the site, uses and activities.

The Site Assessment report includes a discussion of past and present site uses, asbestos, above ground and underground storage tanks, known spills or leaks, waste water discharges and hazardous waste disposal practices, regulatory agency actions, and identification of any visible environmental problems.

The scope of work is not intended to be limited. Penn Environmental will exercise independent judgment as to the significance of data which may be acquired during the course of an investigation.

Once the Site assessment indicates a past use, spill, leak or other confirmation of a release or threat of a release of a hazardous substance at a property, there are a number of different courses of action a property owner can take. Penn Environmental can advise the property owner which course of action will provide the most expeditious and cost- effective solution to a particular environmental problem.

Phase II

A Phase II Investigation may be conducted as a general risk reduction or when prior findings in a Phase I may be cause for additional environmental survey work. Penn Environmental's approach aims to define the scope of the problem, perform the necessary investigative studies, and provide practical, cost-effective recommendations.

The Phase II Investigation is varied and designed to accurately assess a given site. Oftentimes they include collecting samples of subsurface materials for laboratory analysis. If these procedures indicate the presence of hazardous substances, the client may then opt to perform additional investigations in the form of a comprehensive survey. The goal of such a survey is to identify the source and extent of contamination through both soil and groundwater sampling. Included in the final report are procedures and cost estimates for mitigation of hazardous conditions.

Phase III

Phase II investigations sometimes indicate that a site has failed to meet a particular standard required by various regulatory agencies; this situation is often correctable through remedial actions. The remedial work that is required upon completion of a Phase II Investigation is conducted under a Phase III status. A Phase III project is the mitigation of a specific problem at a site and usually involves the remediation and abatement of hazardous materials such as removing leaking underground storage tanks and excavating contaminated soil.

ENVIRONMENTAL SERVICES

Hazardous Material Management

For businesses that handle, sell, store, or use hazardous materials, Penn Environmental registers the materials and obtains the required certificate of registration. This information is particularly helpful in enabling emergency responders to assess and resolve hazardous material incidents quickly and safely. The application process generally aids in reducing the amount of hazardous materials used and waste generated at a particular site.

Designing work plans for the classification, management and cleanup of hazardous materials is critical. Work plans are essential when bidding a job and are normally required in order to obtain permits.

Soil and Groundwater Testing

Soil and groundwater contamination are possible whenever hazardous materials have been used or stored improperly. Penn Environmental's capabilities include comprehensive soil and groundwater contamination studies. Supervision and implementation of testing procedures for soil and groundwater contamination include subsurface soil borings and the installation of monitoring wells.

Underground Storage Tank Management

Underground storage tanks (USTs) were not always as heavily regulated as they are today. Due to the potential for soil and groundwater contamination, explosion hazards, and air pollution, discovery of unknown tanks can result in extensive remediation, activities. Penn Environmental is capable of investigating possible contamination and managing UST remediation projects.

Microbiology Services

Penn Environmental provides a range of services for allergists, home inspectors, safety and health professionals and home owners in the detection of fungi, yeasts, actinomyscetes and bacteria within the living and working environment.

Our services include the sampling and identification of contaminants within an air space, and an interpretation of environmental conditions and their relationship to contaminant levels. Penn Environmental's services also include the remediation of microbial contamination and the establishment of indoor air quality management programs.

SPECIAL REPORT NO. 3 - CONSTRUCTION AND REAL ESTATE CONTRACTS

FROM: Mark Noe

Some matters for you to consider when drafting or reviewing your next construction or property agreement....

PERFORMANCE AND PAYMENT BONDS

Conventional wisdom tells us that owners can reduce their construction risk substantially by bonding their project. **Does bonding provide real and actual risk management reduction? Not on your life!**

If a default occurs, you need to know that it will be <u>at least</u> six [6] months before a bonding company takes over a project, if, in fact, they ever do. The bonding company will use all of its substantial resources to avoid such a calamity as a takeover; including detailed examination of the events leading to the [alleged] default, and scrutinizing the critical elements of the contract's minutiae. I cannot recall a situation....**ever**....where a bonding company took over a project in a timely manner, and completed it with dispatch. In fact, I cannot recall from personal experience within the past decade or so of a bonding company taking over a project. Period.

What to do? First, save the 1-2% [or more] bond premium which the contractor includes as a cost. Second, if there is a truly valid concern about timely completion or payments to vendors and sub-contractors, perhaps the owner should consider hiring another contractor. The low price is not always the best price. And finally, consider hiring a **qualified**, independent construction manager to oversee critical path scheduling requirements, payment authorizations, and project follow-through.

The coup de grace: When a surety takes over a project from a defaulting contractor and completes the work, it stands in the same position the contractor did and is liable for liquidated damages under the contract just as a contractor would have been. [Attorney's Guide to California Construction Contracts and Disputes; James Acret, 2d Ed.]. With this potential, additional liability, a surety surely will not be working at warp speed to cure any default!

LIQUIDATED DAMAGES

What may be said clearly about the law with respect to liquidated damages is that the provisions [Civil Code §1671-81] are seen by many as ambiguous and possibly contradictory.
NOTE: About the only reference to which there appears to be no conflict is with a land purchase agreement which is contingent upon obtaining a future entitlement, such as a tentative sub-division map. With this scenario, a property may be tied up for a couple of years, and yet not have the purchase consummated, with the owner claiming damages.

The definition: Liquidated damages are set when both parties agree that the amount of any damages, such as those caused by delays, will be extremely difficult to determine, and the parties reasonably attempt to estimate fair compensation for any loss which may be sustained. Note also CC §1671(a) "...does **not** apply in any case where another statute expressly applicable to the contract prescribes the rules or standard for determining the validity of a provision in the contract liquidating the damages for the breach of the contract." Generally, a reasonable liquidated damages clause will be valid, unless it appears in a consumer contract or a residential lease: special rules govern real property sales. Finally, liquidated damages cannot be set so as to be construed as a penalty. Penalties are unenforceable in California. An unenforceable penalty **could** be found in many common provisions: security deposit; acceleration clause; late charge.

LIQUIDATED DAMAGES [continued]

Some additional facts:
1.   The burden of proof is upon the party seeking to invalidate a liquidated damages provision. Such proof must show that "the provision was unreasonable under the circumstances existing at the time the contract was made." [CC §1671(b)].
2.   If any of the delays are caused by the owner, this **may** invalidate, or at least apportion, any liquidated damages.
3.   Established folklore says that penalties are enforceable, **provided** that an off-setting completion bonus is included in the contract's provisions. Not true.
4.   It may be argued effectively that **any** to-be-constructed project which will produce income [offices, apartments, etc.] cannot have liquidated damages in that the project's damages are not "extremely difficult to determine", as the projected income and expenses are known, especially if some leases have been executed.

What does all of this mean? As with surety bonds above, if the time schedule is so critical that an owner may be subjected to serious financial loss in not meeting "drop dead" dates, for example, there is no guarantee of getting whole with a liquidated damages provision. A better choice will be to have a construction, design, and management team which has demonstrated past timely completions under all kinds of adverse conditions. Even then, as in any construction project, there will be a risk....acts of God and the like....but the risk will be reduced greatly.

Prepared with the assistance of Charles M. Sink; Farella, Braun & Martel. Mr. Sink is a San Francisco attorney who specializes in construction law and claims.

For additional dialogue on these topics or other construction, real estate, or development matters, please contact:

Mark W. Noe	Charles M. Sink
Sloane Development	Farella, Braun & Martel
Walnut Creek, CA	San Francisco, CA
(925) 939-8707	(415) 954-4400

THE ART OF RESOLVING CONSTRUCTION CLAIMS OR OTHER REAL ESTATE DISPUTES

Most disputes arise because people don't say what they mean; because people don't mean what they say; or because people don't do what they say they will do.

COMMUNICATION
- Educate all parties, especially the owner, regarding construction management, project cost control, value engineering and the potential to avoid liens
- Present to the owner what minimal risk(s) he/she might assume for [a] warranty provisions, as they, practically, have the ultimate risk anyway, and [b] direct vendor payment(s)
- Ensure that the owner understands that there never has been, and maybe never will be, a perfect contract or a set of drawings/specifications. And what the implications of California case law are in this regard
- Refer to sections on agreements as to defusing or avoiding entirely the "change order artist" general contractor or sub-contractor
- Do not expect the other party to change in order to take care of you
- Acknowledge the other party for some quality or action which you appreciate. This will help the other person in listening to you, assuming the acknowledgment is sincere
- Your "truth" may not be as others experience or perceive it. Avoid "judgments". Listen to their feelings and needs and they will listen to yours; again if sincere
- We cannot control the outcome of all situations, even when we communicate well

WIN-WIN NEGOTIATING
- Find out what the other side wants. State what you want. That's the starting point
- Gather as much information as possible on the other side and their needs or situation
- Reach for compromise. Desire to create "win-win" negotiating situations

11 Rules for Win-Win Negotiating
1. Never narrow negotiations down to just one issue. Then there must be a winner and a loser
2. Understand personality styles. The proper mesh of personalities is very critical (see below)
3. Don't fall for "Good Guy/Bad Guy". Then, in effect, the "good guy" is negotiating for you
4. Never say "yes" to the first offer, unless, of course, to do so would be insulting or irrational...or it was what you asked for in the first place. And don't forget to flinch!
5. Always maintain your "Walkaway Power"
6. If an absolute necessity to be the first to name a price, make it flexible
7. **Remember the 80-20 rule.** 80% of concessions are made in the last 20% of the time. The person under the greatest time pressure generally loses. If possible, don't reveal your deadline, and use "Set-Aside" technique to avoid impasse
8. Never offer to split the difference. Have your opponent offer the split to you. Then a lower price already is established, which may be reduced further in the negotiations
9. Confirm the validity of the "Hot Potato". Don't make the problem of another your problem
10. Understand "Body Language" and "Conversational Clues" (auditory, visual and tactile)
11. Confirm "Higher Authority"; the person with whom you are dealing can make the decision

Characteristics of a Successful Negotiation
- Both sides feel sense of accomplishment
- Each side would deal with the other again
- "Winning" ego was removed
- Both sides feel the other cared and was fair
- Each side feels the other will keep the bargain

Generally Accepted Personality Types [#2 above]: Amiable, Extrovert, Pragmatic, Analytical

NOTES

NOTES

NOTES

NOTES

NOTES

NOTES

N OTE S

PROJECT FEASIBILITY - TRUE/FALSE EXAM

1. False	11. False	21. True (3)	31. True
2. True	12. False	22. False	32. True
3. True	13. True	23. True	33. True
4. (1)	14. False	24. False (4)	34. False
5. True	15. True	25. True	35. True
6. False	16. True	26. False	36. True
7. False (2)	17. False	27. False	37. True
8. False	18. True	28. True (5)	38. True
9. False	19. True	29. False (6)	39. False
10. True	20. False	30. True	40. False

MAKING THE DEAL WORK - TRUE/FALSE EXAM

1. True	11. True	21. True	31. False
2. True	12. False	22. False	32. True
3. (7)	13. False	23. False	33. True
4. True	14. False	24. (8)	34. False
5. False	15. True	25. True	35. False
6. True	16. True	26. False	36. True
7. False	17. False	27. True	37. False
8. False	18. True	28. False	38. True
9. False	19. False	29. False	39. False
10. True	20. False	30. (9)	40. False

(1) Could be True or False. Be aware of lender's focus and interest
(2) $1,081,081
(3) Providing Lead Agency allows you to do so
(4) See p. 32
(5) For reasonable lenders who truly want to make construction loans
(6) See p. 17
(7) Could be True or False, depending on your personality and method of doing (successful) business
(8) Could be True or False. Be aware of liability and legal risks
(9) Some counsel do not like binding arbitration; a mediation clause could be a condition precedent to any arbitration, binding or otherwise. True or False

THIS PAGE LEFT BLANK INTENTIONALLY

TO REMOVE TRUE/FALSE ANSWERS
WHEN APPROPRIATE

INDEX

INDEX (Continued)

AFTERWORD

Anyone who has been around this business for more than a couple of days has witnessed examples of or heard horror stories about all types of development or building projects seriously gone awry: "see-through" buildings vacant for years; cost overruns or change orders more than doubling the budget; home renovations which render a home uninhabitable for months and months, or at best, provide the "long term joy of camping out"; pension funds and savings lost; major construction defects which can corral a property (and decrease its value under a cloud of stigma) for years and years in litigation or arbitration whereby the only winners are the attorneys. And it usually does not matter which side they represent.

The tragedy in these real world scenarios is that virtually all of the agony and angst from these traumas could have been avoided. Generally, little attention was paid to the Principles: an impossibly unrealistic budget; poorly crafted construction documents and contracts or agreements; overly optimistic market research; unrealistic financing projections; poor or inept supervisions and inspections. And these are just the highlights, excluding devious partnerships, monumental egos out of control, "creative accounting" and "change order artist" contractors or consultants.

We learn by doing, and your first development, building or renovation project will be the hardest, and there will be some mistakes. Through your study and use of **"GO / NO GO"**, your mistakes should be minor.

Learn as much as you can about the entire business before venturing out and committing your hard-earned dollars (see p. 17: Market Knowledge, not Market Analysis). And do as much as you can yourself staying within your skills and interest. Even in hiring out the balance of the work, be your own best expert for all of the contract documents. No more will you have to say, "I never want to do that again!" about a project. I can't count how many times I have heard that said.

The first step is up to you, and I hope you will take it. There still is very, very good money to be made in development, building and renovation if the project(s) are set up and administered correctly, faithfully following the Principles. Continually refer to **"GO / NO GO"** and make notes (p. 110-116) in it.

And let me know how your projects are progressing, and any ideas how **"GO / NO GO"** may be improved and what topics you would like to see for future study.

Good luck!

Mark Roe

....

BOOK COUPON

BOOK

Thank You!

Please make your check payable to: **REMARK Publishing**
                              Mail to: **P.O. Box 2056**
                                             Sonoma, CA 95476-2056

Quantity _____ **"Go / No Go"** books @ $24.95 ea.   = $_____
              California Residents add 7.5% Sales Tax   =   _____
                              Shipping & Handling   =   2.50
              S & H: Additional Books @ $2.00 ea.   =   _____
                                        TOTAL   = $_____

Name:_____

Company:_____

Address:_____City_____State____Zip_____